American Rose Society

ULTIMATE ROSE

'RINA HUGO'
Hybrid Tea

American Rose Society

ULTIMATE ROSE

'THE LADY'
Hybrid Tea

'FRAGRANT APRICOT'
Floribunda

A Dorling Kindersley Book

Dorling Kindersley

LONDON, NEW YORK, SYDNEY, DELHI, PARIS,
MUNICH, and JOHANNESBURG

'KRISTIN'
Miniature

Editors Beth Smiley, Ray Rogers
Associate Editor Ellen Trice
Designer Carol Wells
DTP Designer Nicola Erdpresser
Production Sara Gordon, Silvia La Greca

Published in the United States by Dorling Kindersley Publishing, Inc.
95 Madison Ave. New York, New York 10016

First American Edition, 2000
2 4 6 8 10 9 7 5 3 1

Dorling Kindersley Books are available at special discounts for bulk purchases for sales promotions or premiums. Special editions,
including personalized covers, excerpts for existing guides, and corporate imprints can be created in large
quantities for specific needs. For more information, contact Special Markets Dept., Dorling Kindersley Publishing, Inc.,
95 Madison Ave., New York, NY 10016; Fax: (800) 600-9098.

Library of Congress Cataloging-in-Publication Data

Ultimate Rose / Beth Smiley, editor and the American Rose Society.—1st American ed.
    p. cm.
ISBN 0-7894-5206-5 (alk. paper)
    1. Roses—Varieties. 2. Rose culture. I. Smiley, Beth. II. American Rose Society.
SB411.6 .U48 2000
635.9'33734--dc21   99-086577

Printed and bound by L. Rex Printing Company Ltd., China.
Color reproduction by GRB Editrice, Verona, Italy.

Front cover 'Glad Tidings'
Front flap 'Valentine Heart' (top)
and 'Tango' (bottom)
Back cover 'Rosa Mundi',
'Nozomi', 'Mountbatten', and
'Gentle Touch' (top)
'Sweet Dream' (bottom)

see our complete catalog at
www.dk.com

'BERRIES 'N' CREAM'
Large-Flowered Climber

'ARTHUR DE SANSAL'
Portland

CONTENTS

'MISS FLIPPINS'
Miniature

'PLAYTIME'
Floribunda

FOREWORD

No other flower is as universally loved and grown or has a more illustrious history than the rose. It is the national floral symbol of at least half a dozen countries, including the United States and England. Grown by themselves or among other plants, roses bring many years of development to bear in an unparalleled array of functionality and beauty. Whether you grow roses for color in the garden, for their beauty and fragrance when cut for the house, for arranging or drying, or simply to give to relatives and friends, a myriad of varieties are available to suit your particular purpose.

This book is a celebration of roses. We at the American Rose Society hope it brings you the joy of experiencing the endless glories of the rose.

Michael C. Kromer
Executive Director
American Rose Society
Shreveport, Louisiana

'JEANNE LAJOIE'
Climbing Miniature

HISTORY OF THE ROSE

The history of the rose stretches back farther than that of mankind itself. Fossil records in various parts of the world have tentatively identified roses as 30 to 40 million years old, and carvings, writings, paintings, and other traces of civilization show evidence of the presence of roses.

In the beginning were the species roses – wild roses that perpetuate themselves naturally.

The discussion of what is and what is not a true species rose is ongoing, but a number somewhere between one to two hundred is now generally agreed upon.

As these species naturally mingled with each other over time, new roses came into existence. While a tidy genealogical record of rose evolution would be wonderful to have, it is unlikely that it will ever be worked out comlpetely. What we can conclude is that a variety of roses, both species and naturally occurring hybrids, were to be found in the Mediterranean region some 2,000 to 3,000 years ago. Whether or not these made their way there from farther East during the conquests of Alexander the Great or through other avenues is probably unknowable.

While various Crusaders are generally credited with bringing new roses back to France and England, it seems just as likely that they slowly made their way north from monastery garden to monastery garden. At the end of the 16th century all the roses known in Europe were once-blooming, meaning they bloom heavily during the late spring and early summer but do not repeat later in the season. During the late 18th century a recurrent-blooming rose, often referred to as 'Autumn Damask', appeared in northern Europe, and by the mid-19th century some 100 varieties of "perpetual" damask were available.

A watershed of rose development occurred in the late 18th century, when species and near-species roses from China began to be introduced into Europe. These roses had the distinctive feature of reblooming, and while they did not thrive in the colder regions of northern Europe, they produced entirely new types of reblooming roses when crossed with the European roses. At that time, breeding or crossing roses consisted of planting different roses in near each other, letting nature do the pollinating, and then harvesting the seed and raising the seedlings. The Englishman Henry Bennett in the 1880s generally gets credit for demonstrating that specific and controlled crosses could more readily result in desired features, but he was likely preceded by some 50 years by the Frenchman Andre Dupont. However, the cooperation between nature

ROSA HUGONIS
(Species)
This rose was sent to Britain in 1899 by Father Hugh Scallon, a missionary to China.

SLATER'S CRIMSON CHINA
(Hybrid China)
Undeniably one of the most important milestones in the hybridizing saga that led to the modern roses was the incorporation of 'Slater's Crimson China' into the bloodlines. See page 40.

DUCHESSE DE BRABANT
(Tea)
President Theodore Roosevelt often wore this very fragrant rose in the lapel of his coat.

and man quickly went forward. The center of this upsurge of rose breeding was the warm region of southern France bordering on the Mediterranean. There, rose seed could be harvested and grown without fear of killing frosts. Records indicate the gardens of the Empress Josephine at Malmaison contained about 260 varieties at her death in 1814. Amazingly, a catalog of Deportes only 15 years later listed some 2,500 varieties, indicating the amount of breeding activity taking place. Recently, the opening of the gardens at Sangerhausen (where a number of older varieties are preserved) in what was formerly East Germany, the finding and cataloging of more than 100 varieties of hybrid spinosissimas (Scotch roses) in the wild during the last decade, the preservation efforts of "rose rustlers" in the American Southwest, and other such activities all bode well for the continuation of the old garden, or heritage, varieties.

Hybrid teas are the oldest and still the most popular family of what is referred to as modern roses. Originally crosses between hybrid perpetuals and teas, they now carry the bloodlines of many other rose classes. The rose 'La France', hybridized by Guillot, has been retrospectively (and somewhat arbitrarily) declared the first hybrid tea, and its 1867 date of introduction represents the line of demarcation between old roses and modern roses. The breeding of hybrid teas flourished in the early part of the 20th century, languished somewhat during the 1930s and the war years, and caught fire with the introduction of the incomparable 'Peace' in 1945. Since then they have become the virtual hallmark of the genus *Rosa*.

While the hybrid teas were preparing to usher in the 20th century, plant hunters were combing the far reaches of Asia to close out the 19th. Since the late 1700s plantsmen from gardens and arboretums all over Europe had been mining the wealth of hitherto unknown species roses to be found in China and the rest of east Asia, a few of which would have a major impact on rose development.

PEACE
(Hybrid Tea)
Some people divide rose history into two periods: Before 'Peace' and After 'Peace'. Also see pages 79 and 108.

When gardeners in the future look back on the rose as it evolved during the 20th century, what will they see? It is likely they will look at the large class known somewhat generically as shrubs as an area of considerable change that brings old rose bloom and bush form into the present through incorporation of remontancy and increased fragrance. Also, during the last three or four decades miniature roses have truly come into their own.

'AUSTRALIA'S OLYMPIC GOLD ROSE'
(Grandiflora)
Named in honor of the Sydney 2000 Olympic Summer Games and taking roses into the 21st century, this represents the culmination of centuries of effort to produce new roses for gardeners everywhere.

As gardens become smaller with increasing population density, there is more demand for roses that can be grown in containers and other restricted areas. One thing of which we can be certain is that changes in the roses we grow, perhaps through genetic engineering in the not-too-distant future, are inevitable.

ROSES IN OUR LIVES

No survey of the history of the rose would be complete without looking at its "footprints" in the course of civilization. These indicate the presence and appreciation of the rose in various societies during the course of the last three centuries, but they do not necessarily point to specific rose varieties or families as the point of reference. It is often counterproductive to try to assign specific varieties to the "rose of Paestum," the "Rose of Sharon," or roses included in many literary and artistic works. Such attempts will invariably involve speculation, but more importantly they detract from the real import of these appearances: a familiarity and knowledge of roses among both the author/artist and, presumably, the audience. We can appreciate the psalmist's expression of youth, beauty, and the joy of life in the symbolism of a rose without knowing what specific rose, if any, was intended.

'ALBA SEMI-PLENA'
(Alba)
The albas are an ancient class of rose and appear frequently in art and, in a more idealized form, in fabric designs. Also see page 24.

Other than passing references in the works of Homer and Sappho, one of the first writings to deal extensively with the rose is Anacreon's Ode 51, written sometime in the 5-6th century B.C. This lyric poem treats the mythological creation of the rose in association with the birth of Aphrodite (Venus), the same theme taken up by Boticelli in *The Birth of Venus*. One particularly illustrative verse (in a translation by Mrs. Herbert Hills) reads:

This flower takes off diseases,
In sickness greatly pleases;
Its old age cannot sever
The scent it loses never;
And dead, we keep forever
The perfumed air
of roses fair.

'APOTHECARY'S ROSE'
(Species)
The name is a reflection of the herbal importance of this rose It has been used for centuries to treat a wide range of ailments.

The rose is mentioned seven times in the King James version of the Bible, twice in the Old Testament and five times in the Apocrypha, a section not included in some versions of the Protestant and Jewish scriptures. However, later versions of the Bible that pursue a more strict translation of the Greek, Hebrew, and Aramaic texts change most of these wordings to indicate a general or specific flowering plant other than the rose. Rather than take this to mean that roses were not present in the eastern Mediterranean in biblical times (since other evidence shows conclusively that they were), a more realistic view would be that the rose was so familiar to the English scholars and translators of the 17th century that they felt correct in inserting it as a recognizable symbol of beauty. In the 13th century a long allegorical poem called "Roman de la Rose" ("Romance of the Rose") appeared in France. Started by Guillaume de Lorris and finished by Jean de Meun, it was immensely popular for some three centuries and tells of a lover paying court to his lady (the rose) and encountering various impediments (thorns) along the way; the swain attempts to pick a beautiful bud but is driven back by the thorns. This use of the rose to symbolize the beautiful as well as the painful aspects of life is seen also in Omar Khayyam's famous "Rubiyat" from the 12th century, wherein the subject is not the pursuit of love but rather the admonition to live life to the fullest while we can. The rose is mentioned in 9 of the 90 stanzas of the "Rubiyat" and represents not only life, youth, and springtime but also their inevitable passing:

Oh come with old Khayyam
and leave the wise
To talk; one thing is certain,
that time flies;
One thing is certain, and
the rest is lies;
The rose that once has blown
forever dies.

The rose as a symbol of the all-too-swift passing of youth and beauty has been echoed by any number of poets and may be represented by the famous opening line of Robert Herrick's *To Virgins To Make Much of Time*: "Gather ye rosebuds while ye may…" The rose becomes the metaphor for life itself: a thing of beauty but also filled with thorns, it opens to its fullness all to quickly and then is gone, only to be replaced by new generations.

A ROSE BATTLE

Perhaps the rose's most famous historical occurrence is also its most problematic, bordering on legend rather than historical fact. Fifteenth-century England's War of the Roses between the houses of Lancaster and York, in which the two used a red rose and a white rose, respectively, as their badge or symbol, is often taken literally with regard to the roses. The notion that the Lancastrians used or wore a real rose, usually considered to be 'Apothecary's Rose' (a deep pink gallica also known as *R. gallica officinalis* and "The Red Rose of Lancaster"), while the Yorkists countered with the 'White Rose of York' (also known as *Rosa* x *alba*), owes more to Shakespeare's *Henry VI, Part I* than it does to historical truth. In fact, a heraldic five-petaled rose, probably based on one of the many species roses native to England, had been used by the Plantaganet monarchs for at least a few centuries. Various personages used different colors in the rose; Edward I had a golden rose as his badge, and other

HERO (Shrub)
Shakespearean names inspire rose hybridizers: here is a character from *Much Ado About Nothing*.

'ROSA MUNDI'
(Species)
This sport of 'Apothecary's Rose' (see the previous page) has graced gardens for more than 500 years.

heraldic colors such as azure had also appeared. Lancaster and York's use of red and white merely carried on the heraldic tradition. The Tudor Rose of Henry VII, uniting the houses of Lancaster and York with a small white rose placed inside a red one, is similarly a purely symbolic and heraldic creation.

INTO TODAY

During World War II, interference with trade cut off England's supply of citrus fruits, a primary dietary source of Vitamin C. With the country's children beginning to show early signs of scurvy, the search began to find an alternate source of this vital nutrient. It was discovered that the hips of wild roses growing naturally in hedgerows across the country provided 24 to 36 times more vitamin C than orange juice and 60 times more than lemons. Rose hips were also found to provide vitamins A, B, E, K, and P as well as phosphorus, calcium, and niacin. Harvesting across the countryside provided the hips needed to make tea, soup, and a syrup given to English children. Rose hips are still used today for medicinal purposes.

CLASSIFYING ROSES

Genus Rosa

Species roses

Species (Sp)

Old Garden Roses

Alba (A)
Ayshire (Ayr)
Bourbon and Climbing Bourbon (B & Cl B)
Boursalt (Bslt)
Centifolia (C)
Damask (D)
Hybrid Bracteata (HBc)
Hybrid China & Climbing Hybrid China (HCh & Cl HCh)
Hybrid Eglanteria (HEg)
Hybrid Foetida (HFt)
Hybrid Gallica (HGal)
Hybrid Multiflora (HMulti)
Hybrid Perpetual & Climbing Hybrid Perpetual (HP & Cl HP)
Hybrid Sempervirens (HSem)
Hybrid Setigera (HSet)
Hybrid Spinosissima (HSpn)
Miscellaneous Old Garden Roses (Misc. OGR)
Moss & Climbing Moss (M & Cl M)
Noisette (N)
Portland (P)
Tea & Climbing Tea (T & Cl T)

ROSA RUGOSA ALBA
Species (page 14)

'MME PIERRE OGER'
Bourbon (page 28)

'TUSCANY'
Hybrid Gallica (page 42)

'CÉLINE FORESTIER'
Noisette (page 60)

Modern Roses

Floribunda & Climbing Floribunda (F & Cl F)
Grandiflora & Climbing Grandiflora (Gr & Cl Gr)
Hybrid Kordesii (HKor)
Hybrid Moyesii (HMoy)
Hybrid Musk (HMsk)
Hybrid Rugosa (HRg)
Hybrid Wichurana (HWich)
Hybrid Tea & Climbing Hybrid Tea (HT & Cl HT)
Large-flowered Climber (LCl)
Miniature & Climbing Miniature (Min & Cl Min)
Mini-Flora (MinFl)
Polyantha & Climbing Polyantha (Pol & Cl Pol)
Shrub (S)

Building on landmark achievements including Darwin's work on the origin of species, Mendel's experiments in genetics, and Linnaeus' development of a common naming system, science has studied the family relationships among all organisms. From the most general categorization as either "plant" or "animal," down to the basic levels of species and variety, zoologists and botanists attempt to organize all living things into systems of classification. The study of the kinds and diversity of organisms, along with their interrelationships, is called systematics. Taxonomy is the discipline within systematics that focuses on devising systems of classification; these systems are intended to divide organisms into groups (taxa) based on a set of defined characteristics that is shared by all members of a given group. When developing a classification system that recognizes groupings and is useful to botanists, hybridizers, commercial nurserymen, and gardeners, many different perspectives must be reconciled. Such a system must retain its scientific basis, but it must also allow the rose gardener to visit his local retailer and assume that, should he purchase a floribunda, he will get a repeat-blooming rose that bears its flowers in clusters, grows as a moderate-sized, bushy plant, and requires winter protection in colder climates, similar to other floribundas. Furthermore, the system must recognize that the strictly botanical methodology and terminology that is appropriate to species roses and some old garden roses is not suitable for other old garden roses and complex modern hybrids. The American Rose Society classification system presented here attempts to satisfy all of the above requirements. However, ongoing study and modification of this system illustrates the inherent nature of all classification systems. They are not meant to be static and unchanging but instead must remain flexible enough to incorporate the latest developments and available knowledge about the type of plant being studied. As the International Registration Authority for Roses, the American Rose Society bears the additional responsibility for gathering educated opinions from around the world and incorporating them where appropriate. Different classification systems are in use by other members of the World Federation of Rose Societies, and it remains a challenge to improve consistency among the various approaches.

'BLUEBERRY HILL'
Floribunda (page 80)

'QUAKER STAR'
Grandiflora (page 88)

'ELINA'
Hybrid Tea (page 104)

'SCHOOLGIRL'
Large-flowered Climber
(page 116)

SPECIES ROSES

Species roses are the progenitors – the wild roses – created by nature. Their fossil records date back some 30 to 40 million years, and roses have been found naturally dispersed or growing wild in virtually all areas of the Northern Hemisphere but not, interestingly, in the Southern, although they do thrive there. Geography plays an additional role in the examination of species roses in that point of origin provides one of the simplest methods of subdividing the group for study. Four regions (North America, Europe, the Middle East, and Oriental Asia) are considered the natural divisions in studying the origins of species roses. North America, for example, is home to about a dozen species roses, including *Rosa blanda*, *Rosa setigera* (see page 20), and *Rosa nitida*, plus some that carry recognizable place names such as *Rosa carolina*, *Rosa californica*, and *Rosa virginiana*. Botanists still debate what exactly constitutes a species rose and how many there actually are, but somewhere between one to two hundred is generally agreed upon. Species roses are mostly medium to large shrubs. Most have five-petaled blooms, although some (such as *Rosa roxburghii* on page 16 and *Rosa banksiae lutea* on page 18) have more petals, and one (*Rosa sericea*) has only four. Their bloom is often sparse especially when compared with many of today's modern roses. Many are once-blooming, also in contrast to many modern roses, but many other garden shrubs bloom only once, so do consider adding some species roses to your garden.

Species roses make useful garden specimens, not only on account of their blooms, but also on their other interesting features, such as the blue-gray foliage of *Rosa glauca* (see page 20), the glistening red thorns of *Rosa sericea pteracantha*, the distinctive flaking bark of *Rosa roxburghii*, and the brightly colored hips of *Rosa canina* (see page 156) and many other species.

ROSA EGLANTERIA
The sweetbriar rose. This species' leaves smell like cooking apples, especially on a misty day.

BRINGING SPECIES ROSES TOGETHER

How one to two hundred species resulted in the literally thousands of roses that exist today is a matter of simple genetics, with a significant helping hand from man. All roses, especially species roses, display varying traits. For example, the species roses originating in the Middle East are often yellow, while those found in Europe bloom primarily in shades of white and pink. Some roses from Oriental Asia bloom more than once per season, while roses from most other parts of the world do not. Through pollination by bees and other insects, the mixing of traits occurred naturally among roses growing near one another, and roses with different combinations of characteristics emerged.

As commerce brought the world together, the exchange of plants among enthusiasts and the products of plant-hunting expeditions to previously unaccessible parts of the world provided more opportunities for new roses to come into being. Also, the creation of new roses became more predictable and sophisticated as rosarians moved from the unreliable method of planting potential rose parents close to each other in the garden to the more complicated processes of intentional cross pollination. Through these means, roses could be bred with the hope that they would display specific traits such repeat blooming or a specific color.

NAMING SPECIES ROSES

Species roses all carry Latin (or Latinized) names or synonyms and are the only plants called roses to be named *Rosa* legitimately. Their names may relate to their discovers (for example, *Rosa wichurana* after Max Wichura or *Rosa hugonis* after Father Hugo), to their place of origin (such as *Rosa chinensis* of China, or *Rosa palustris* of swamps), or to some

ROSA CAROLINA
Spreads by suckers to form a low hedge.

feature of their plant or flower (including *Rosa multiflora*, meaning many flowered, or *Rosa rubrifolia*, meaning red foliaged).

EXPLORING FOR SPECIES ROSES

Tales of the wealth and beauty of China intrigued Europeans from the time of Marco Polo, but with navigation still in its infancy, simply reaching this part of the world proved virtually impossible until the 17th and 18th centuries. Once the challenges of rounding the African continent were met, the hostile Chinese government, not open to the infiltration of European trade, proved to be the next hurdle to overcome.

Slowly, areas were opened to entities such as the English East India Company and its competitor, the Dutch East India Company, which were primarily concerned with the quest for tea, silks, spices, and other commodities. However, representatives of these companies often gathered seeds of many plants, including roses, and live plants were sometimes shipped back to European gardeners as well. By the 1840s, five Chinese ports had been

opened to trade, but the interior of the country remained off limits. It was about this time that botanist Robert Fortune was hired by the Royal Botanic Gardens in Kew, England and the East India Company specifically to bring back plants and seed from China. Like other traders, Fortune was restricted to nurseries, temple grounds, and private gardens near the port cities. Seeking to travel outside these areas, Fortune is said to have donned native dress, shaved his head leaving only enough hair for a hand-fashioned queue (the traditional Chinese braid) to be attached, and hired a Chinese servant.Thus disguised he traveled secretly into the Chinese interior, gathering numerous garden plants and several roses for return to Europe. Three roses – 'Fortune's Double Yellow', 'Fortune's Five Colored Rose' and *Rosa anemoneflora* – are credited to Fortune, but it is not clear if the rose now known as 'Fortuniana' was found by the explorer or simply named in his honor. Fortune penned four books chronicling his adventures into "Fe-tee" (the Flowering Land). Through the efforts of Robert Fortune and other plant hunters, the late 18th and and early 19th centuries saw a great increase in known species as China and other areas of eastern Asia became open to western horticulturists. Although it is possible that one or two species roses may have still eluded the detection of plant explorers, the genus now seems to be complete.

Species roses are more than just historical curiosities or links to our past. With their multiplicity of plant features and bloom forms and colors, they constitute another facet in the rose spectrum available to today's gardeners.

OTHER SPECIES ROSES

This book includes a sampling of the species roses of the world. Others (not pictured) include:

- *Rosa arkansana*
- *Rosa blanda*
- *Rosa californica*
- *Rosa gigantea*
- *Rosa gymnocarpa*
- *Rosa laxa*
- *Rosa longicuspis*
- *Rosa nitida*
- *Rosa palustris*
- *Rosa primula*
- *Rosa sempervirens*
- *Rosa soulieana*
- *Rosa stellata*
- *Rosa villosa*

ROSA CANINA
The dog rose of Europe is featured in John William Hill's *Bird's Nest and Dog Roses*.

LEFT TO RIGHT, TOP TO BOTTOM

ROSA NUTKANA
Growing naturally from Northern California to Alaska, the Nootka rose produces pink flowers followed by plump, bright red hips.

ROSA SPINOSISSIMA LUTEA
This is a color variant of the burnet rose, which grows from eastern Europe to Korea. It is in the lineage of several modern shrub roses.

ROSA RUGOSA ALBA
Known as the Japanese rose or the sea tomato (after the size and color of its hips), the species and its color variants, including this white one, have given rose to an entire class of rose, the hybrid rugosas (see page 100). Native to eastern Russia, Korea, Japan, and northern China, this species has naturalized throughout much of Great Britain and eastern North America. The hips, rich in vitamin C, were collected in England during World War II as part of the war effort and made into a healthy drink.

ROSA ROXBURGHII
Appropriately known as the chestnut rose, this bears prickly calyxes and hips that resemble chestnut burrs. A taxonomic oddity, this is the double-flowered form of the single-flowered (five-petaled) botanical variety *normalis* from Western China. Apparently, the double form was introduced from Chinese gardens and named before the single form was found. As a result, the single form, normally the entity bearing a two-part scientific name, is considered a variant of the double form, which normally bears a three-part name derived from the two-part name of the species.

ROSA GALLICA
Here is one color variant of the ancestor of the hybrid gallicas (see page 42) as well as of many of the European old garden roses and some modern roses. Commonly known as the French or red rose, it grows naturally from central and southern Europe to Turkey and Iraq, and it also has escaped from cultivation and now grows wild in parts of eastern North America.

'ROSA MUNDI'
When pressed for the one rose to grow to the exclusion of all others, some rose growers give their endorsement to 'Rosa Mundi'. Although it blooms only once per season, few other roses can equal the spectacular display of this variant of *Rosa gallica*. The true history of its importation into gardens is unknown.

'GREEN ROSE' ABOVE
The flowers of this curiosity are composed entirely of sepals, the green flower parts that normally occur as the five triangular coverings for the petals in a rosebud. Flower arrangers take note: the flowers last an amazingly long time in water. 'Green Rose' may have arisen from *Rosa chinensis*.

'KIFTSGATE' RIGHT
Perhaps the largest-growing rose in the world, a plant of 'Kiftsgate' in the garden at Kiftsgate Court in England is reputed to have engulfed and destroyed a large, old beech tree. This is sometimes considered as a form of *Rosa filipes*, a Himalayan (western China) species.

ROSA BANKSIAE LUTEA FAR RIGHT TOP
Also known as "Yellow Lady Banks," this is treasured in warm climates around the world. A less fragrant color variant of *Rosa banksiae* from western and central China, it climbs strongly and blooms more freely than the species or its other variants. The species name honors the wife of Sir Joseph Banks. He was one of the more highly regarded directors of the Royal Botanic Gardens in Kew, England.

ROSA BRACTEATA FAR RIGHT BOTTOM
The common name of Macartney rose recalls Lord Macartney, whose secretary, Sir George Staunton, discovered this rose while on a mission to China. A plant later sent to Thomas Jefferson was the first plant of what would become many acres of this rose growing in the southeastern United States. Whether an erosion-controlling blessing or a land-eating curse, few dispute the beauty of the flowers of this species. Leafy bracts surround the flower, giving it is specific name.

ROSA FOETIDA AND ROSA FOETIDA BICOLOR
ABOVE AND RIGHT TOP AND MIDDLE

The species name of the Austrian yellow rose, originally from Asia, refers to its (to some) unpleasant, or fetid, flower scent. The *bicolor* variant, commonly called the Austrian copper rose, bears flowers whose petals are a startling orange-red on top and yellow underneath. Plants of *Rosa foetida bicolor* frequently revert (mutate) back, often just a branch or two, and they then produce the yellow flowers of *Rosa foetida*, as above.

ROSA BANKSIAE BANKSIAE RIGHT BOTTOM

This is often the first rose of spring in warmer climates, perfuming the air with the scent of violets. Also see *Rosa banksiae lutea* on page 18.

ROSA LAEVIGATA FAR RIGHT TOP

The evergreen foliage and rather large flowers of the Cherokee rose make this vigorously climbing species an attractive addition to large gardens. Native to southeast Asia, it has widely naturalized in the southeastern US.

'MUTABILIS' FAR RIGHT MIDDLE

The single flowers of this relative of *Rosa chinensis* change from yellow to pink to crimson as they age, giving the illusion that the shrub is covered with butterflies.

ROSA RUGOSA RUBRA FAR RIGHT BOTTOM

This form of *Rosa rugosa,* like many of its kin, produces clove-scented flowers that give way to showy, large red hips. Also see *Rosa rugosa alba*, page 16.

ROSA SETIGERA EXTREME RIGHT TOP

The Prairie rose from eastern and central North America is the parent of the hybrid setigeras (see page 74).

ROSA GLAUCA EXTREME RIGHT BOTTOM

Distinctive purplish red foliage and contasting pink flowers distinguish this native of central and southern Europe.

OLD GARDEN ROSES

"Everything old is new again" may be a song lyric, but it is a refrain that can certainly be applied to the current resurgence of interest in old garden roses (OGRs), also called heritage roses. As is man's wont, the old is often pushed aside for the new, and that is what occurred with old garden roses when the hybrid tea class was developed in the 1860s. Suddenly, the soft and elegant blooms of old garden roses were being upstaged by the more vibrant hues of hybrid teas whose classic long-stemmed buds lent themselves more readily to cutting and arranging. Appealing, too, were the recurrent (multiple) bloom cycles of the newer roses.

As more modern classes evolved, old garden roses were pushed farther into the background, to the point where many varieties were lost to cultivation.

It is a clear testament to their hardiness that so many survived and were either rescued by gardening preservationists or survived in old cemeteries, private estates, and old homesites until they could be "discovered" and admired by a new generation.

These are the roses that inspired classical poets and musicians. They are the roses used as symbols of war and the ones portrayed by artists in great masterpieces. Their images were woven into tapestries and patterned by artisans into everything from urns to silverware to china. Their fragrance has inspired perfumers, but it is elusive – and exclusive – to the rose and has never been truly replicated.

Roses have been around since time immemorial, but with travel limited and the civilized world being constricted by wars and hazards of both nature and conveyance, countries were unaware not only of each other but of the roses flourishing in different parts of the world. Europeans were familiar only with damasks, albas, gallicas, centifolias, mosses, and various species roses, unaware that many

'GLOIRE DE DIJON'
(Climbing Tea)
Superlatives are used to describe this presumed child of the bourbon rose 'Souv de la Malmaison' (see pages 28 and 30).

other roses were thriving in other parts of the world. It wasn't until the 18th century, when China briefly opened its doors for tea trading, that the remontant tea and china classes were brought to Europe. Their cultivation and resultant hybridization with the aforementioned European roses truly put the boom into the rose world, expanding the classes and availability of roses to the masses.

Plant explorers traveled great distances and encountered many perils, all to procure different roses from the farthest-flung corners of the world. Indeed, for them to be so desired, praised, and portrayed, there must be something truly special about the old garden roses.

Many old garden roses are not demanding in that they do not demand visual attention. They may not have the flash of modern roses, but what they do have is staying power and the ability to blend quietly into the landscape, for they are truly the original "landscape" rose. There is a type of old garden rose to fit every gardening need, from container subject, to specimen, to climber, to bedding plant. Many are more disease resistant than most modern roses, and most require minimal pruning. Their blooms range from the delicate to the full-bodied

'REINE DES VIOLETTES'
(Hybrid Perpetual)
The "Queen of the Violets" belongs to one of the groups that directly led to the hybrid teas (page 104).

'MARÉCHAL NIEL' (Noisette)
Noisettes are treasured in warmer regions for their
production of sherbet-colored, fragrant blooms.
See page 62.

"cabbagey," with a color spectrum from white to the most delicate shell pink, to the darkest of purples, and the palest of yellows, to the roguish red. To walk through a garden of old garden roses in bloom is to experience a veritable feast of fragrance that can only be described as intoxicating.

Enjoying the fragrance or the old garden roses is the original aromatherapy. To catch their scent on soft spring these roses. The variety we so admire today could very well have originated from a bush some 100 or more years ago in a land thousands of miles away. The old garden roses are indeed very evocative flowers. It is no wonder, then, that these aristocrats of the genus *Rosa* have endured long enough for the world to reawaken and acknowledge again their rightful place in the landscape and the heart.

PRESERVING OLD GARDEN ROSES

Old garden roses were once popular in the cottage gardens and estates of the 18th and 19th centuries, where they flourished as treasured landscape plants and exhibition favorites. Over the years, they were replaced in people's hearts and gardens by the modern roses, so they gradually faded into obscurity. As still more time passed, gardeners began to rediscover the appeal of the old roses, so many "oldies" were resurrected from old gardens and reintroduced into commerce. Commonly referred to as "rose rustling," this practice continues to the present day. Albeit rather illicit-sounding, rose rustling is actually admirable in its scope. Rustlers scout out plants around old cemeteries, in overgrown yards of abandoned homes, and in the gardens of green-thumbed homeowners with a bent toward collecting and growing anything and everything – including Grandma's rose. They try to preserve the plant in its natural surroundings, which sometimes means weeding or trimming other overgrown plants. Some roses found by rustlers are propagated and distributed in commercial and noncommercial channels. Although their original names may never be known, the roses found and rescued by rustlers continue to please rose lovers as they did when they were brand new.

• For more information on rose rustlers and other groups interested in growing and preserving old garden roses, see the Acknowledgments on page 160.

mornings evokes memories of slower times and gives one pause to imagine and perhaps remember those gentler images of a bygone era. The rose that was growing on the porch at Great-Grandma's could very well be the same one that smells so sweetly in your rose-growing friend's garden now.

These roses made their way across oceans, continents, and mountains in the form of cuttings that were preciously guarded and preserved until they could take root in their new home. It is no wonder, then, that such a rose could possess such power, for as each person has a story, so, too, do many of

'CABBAGE ROSE'
(Centifolia)
This rose, known in cultivation since 1596, is the prototype for its class (see page 32). The class name literally means "hundred leaf," referring to the abundant petals found in the blooms of many varieties. Cabbage roses have been the subjects of floral painters, textile designers, and greeting-card manufacturers for centuries.

ALBA

It is believed the albas arose from a cross between a gallica rose (see page 42) and *Rosa canina*, the dog rose (see page 15). The early albas were popular among European rosarians, who enjoyed the fragrance of their semidouble to double blooms, and the English House of York chose an alba as its heraldic symbol. Members of this class are once-blooming in late spring or early summer, and the typically blue-green or gray-green leaves serve as a complement to the white, cream, and pastel pink blooms. Bushes are robust, and some varieties will attain the height of 8 to 10ft (2.5 to 2.8m). Many are resistant to the common rose diseases and, as a group, are more tolerant of light to moderate shade than most other classes of old garden rose.

'CELESTIAL'
Also commonly known as "Celeste," the petals of this vigorous 5ft (1.5m) rose are almost translucent.

'GREAT MAIDEN'S BLUSH' OPPOSITE PAGE
Considered one of the finest of all the old garden roses, this rose weighs down the long, arching branches on which it blooms. It can be described as a larger version of 'Maiden's Blush' (see left).

'MAIDEN'S BLUSH'
Although smaller in stature than 'Great Maiden's Blush', this rose is just as fragrant and seductive.

'ALBA SEMI-PLENA'
Albas were popular among artists who included roses in their works. The roses depicted in Botticelli's painting "Birth of Venus" are most probably 'Alba Semi-plena'.

LEFT TO RIGHT, TOP TO BOTTOM

'MME PLANTIER'
This was grown by the renowned author and gardener
Vita Sackville-West at her world-famous garden at
Sissinghurst Castle in Kent, England

'MME LEGRAS DE ST GERMAIN'
Given proper support, this variety will climb attractively.

'FÉLICITÉ PARMENTIER'
The Parmentiers were a prominent French family of
plant hybridizers in the early 19th century.

'BELLE AMOUR'
Apparently lost to cultivation for some time, 'Belle
Amour' was rediscovered at a Norman convent in 1940
and then reintroduced into general cultivation.

'KÖNIGIN VON DÄNEMARK'
The most vibrantly colored of the albas. The name
means "Queen of Denmark."

'WHITE ROSE OF YORK'
Made famous in English history by the House of York
selecting it as its heraldic symbol. This may be the same
as 'Alba Semi-plena' (see page 24).

'ALBA MAXIMA'
Among its many other names are "Cheshire Rose,"
"Great Double White," "Maxima," and "The Jacobite
Rose," reflecting this rose's long history.

BOURBON

The first bourbons came into being as a result of a natural cross between a china rose ('Old Blush', see page 40) and 'Autumn Damask' (see page 36), which were growing intermixed in hedgerows on the Ile de Bourbon (now Réunion) in the Indian Ocean. This class achieved its height of popularity in the mid 19th century, and in recent years its popularity appears to be on the rise again. The bourbons' pedigree is complex and frequently has been divided into subgroups. For example, some bourbons express their china rose ancestry by displaying slender, flexible canes and blooms typical of the chinas, while others display their damask background through their stout canes and associated bloom form. Many varieties provide reliable recurrent (repeat) bloom production, while some bourbons will seldom repeat. They are generally less winter hardy than hybrid perpetuals (see page 50).

'SOUV DE LA MALMAISON'
Named for the home of Napoleon's Empress Josephine, this is considered one of the best of its class. See page 30 for its more usual pink coloration

'LOUISE ODIER' OPPOSITE PAGE
This rose was frequently used in French hybridizing programs. It shows the lush, full form typical of many roses in this class.

'MME ISAAC PERÉIRE'
This rose bears the name of the wife of a Parisian banker in business during the reign of Napoleon III.

LEFT TO RIGHT, TOP TO BOTTOM

'VARIEGATA DI BOLOGNA'
This tall grower occasionally sports back to its parent 'Victor Emmanuel' to produce solid-colored flowers without markings.

'ZÉPHIRINE DROUIHN'
Unike other roses that make the claim, it's thornless! Use this rose on a pillar or arbor that sees heavy traffic, such as by a doorway or in a busy garden/

'BOULE DE NEIGE'
Its name means "snowball," which is just what the cupped blooms resemble. The pure white color is accentuated by dark green foliage.

'HONORINE DE BRABANT'
Its namesake and origin are a mystery. The appeal of its striped and spotted blooms is not.

'SOUV DE LA MALMAISON'
Named for the home of Napoleon and his Empress Josephine. See page 28 for a picture that shows the apricot tones the flowers take on when grown in a mild climate such as that found in England.

'MME PIERRE OGER'
This delicate creation was named for the mother of Norman explorer M. A. Oger. It sported from the famous 'La Reine Victoria', a rich pink Bourbon.

'MME ERNEST CALVAT'
A sport of Mme Isaac Pereire (see page 28), discovered and introduced by the widow of hybridizer J. Schwartz.

CENTIFOLIA

In the absence of reliable records regarding the origins of the 'Cabbage Rose', the matriarch of this class, it remained for modern cytological (cell-structure) studies to determine that it is a complex hybrid rather than a species. It is known that much of the early hybridizing of the centifolias was carried out during the 16th and 17th centuries by the Dutch. The fragrant blooms are nonrecurrent, globe-shaped, and very double, thus creating the "100-petaled" appearance. Because of the large petal count and weak peduncles, the usually pink blooms tend to droop. The sepals are characteristically long, frequently covered with glands. The bushes of this class are usually large and sprawling, with arching canes bearing coarsely toothed foliage and a mixture of large and small prickles.

'PETITE DE HOLLANDE'
Here is an old garden rose suitable for growing in containers: small blooms are borne in clusters on a plant of moderate size.

'TOUR DE MALAKOFF' OPPOSITE PAGE
The flower's vivid magenta coloration fades to a gentler lilac-gray as it ages.

'FANTIN - LATOUR'
Named for the 19th century French artist famous for his still-life paintings, this rose can be grown next to a low-branched spring-flowering tree. Given some initial support, it will in time clamber into the tree to provide another season of bloom.

DAMASK

With abundant reports regarding the popularity of damasks among the citizens of the Roman Empire, this class of rose is considered to be one of the most ancient among the old garden roses. The intensely fragrant, semidouble to double blooms are generally white or pink, are produced in small clusters, and are generally found atop short peduncles. Some varieties have a characteristic "pip," or button, in the bloom's center. With few exceptions, damasks are nonrecurrent. Many damask varieties produce large bushes with stout canes and dense prickles, but some, such as 'Rose de Rescht', have a stature similar to hybrid teas and floribundas. The leaves of the winter-hardy bushes are large, grayish green, and velvety soft with deeply toothed margins.

'CELSIANA'
Often featured in the works of Dutch painter Van Huysum, 'Celsiana' gently fades to almost white (see the other picture on page 36).

'ISPAHAN' OPPOSITE PAGE
Its name recalls the former capital of Persia. The city was filled with roses, but it is not known if 'Ispahan' grew there.

'ROSE DE RESCHT'
Unusually dark in color for a damask, this rose was rediscovered and reintroduced into cultivation by English writer Nancy Lindsay in the 1940s.

LEFT TO RIGHT, TOP TO BOTTOM

'AUTUMN DAMASK'

Probably the reblooming "Four Season's Rose of Paestum" mentioned by classical writers, this rose has been known by many names over the centuries, including "Rose des Quatre Saisons," "Rose of Castile," and *Rosa damascena semperflorens*.

'CELSIANA'

Beginning as a deeper pink (see page 34), the blooms of 'Celsiana' gracefully fade to white with just a hint of pink.

'LA VILLE DE BRUXELLES'

Although bred in France, it is named for the Belgian capital of Brussels. It can grow to five feet or more if given support and appropriate pruning.

'MME HARDY'

Rose breeder Eugene Hardy named this rose in honor of his wife in 1832. It is still considered one of the finest white roses ever produced. Of special interest is the green "eye" in the center of the carefully arranged petals.

'KAZANLIK'

This rose is grown by the acre in Europe for obtaining rose attar, the thick, oily substance highly prized by perfume makers. It is distilled from the flowers in much the same way as was done centuries ago.

'LÉDA'

Also called the "Painted Damask," this button-eyed classic is named for the mythological maiden queen who was seduced by Zeus while he was in the form of a swan.

'MARIE LOUISE'

Although this rose originated at Malmaison, the garden of Napoleon's first wife Empress Josephine, it is named for the Emperor's second wife.

HYBRID CHINA

The china roses are arguably the Far East's greatest contribution to the rose world. They bloom throughout summer, in contrast to the once- blooming old garden roses of European origin. When these two classes were brought together, their resulting progeny displayed the highly prized characteristic of repeat blooming. The chinas' single-petaled or semidouble blooms usually possess little fragrance and are produced in clusters. The flowers of many chinas go through attractive color changes as they age, often darkening dramatically. Although there are climbing chinas, most are short bushes reaching 3 to 4ft (1 to 1.2m) tall. Their delicate, slender canes bear small, glossy, light green leaves. The plants are moderately disease resistant, and their cold hardiness is slightly less than that of hybrid teas and floribundas. Many chinas make good choices for growing in containers, especially in colder areas.

'HERMOSA'
Some students of rose classification feel this is more closely related to the bourbons (see page 28). It superficially resembles 'Old Blush' (see page 40), but its flowers have more petals and the plant is more compact.

'CRAMOISI SUPÉRIEUR'
"Cramoisi" is the French word for the color crimson. This rose escaped from cultivation and now grows naturally in Bermuda.

'PINK PET'
Introduced much later than
many hybrid chinas (in 1928),
the blooms of 'Pink Pet'
are small, flat, and very double
with a button center.

LEFT TO RIGHT, TOP TO BOTTOM

'POMPON DE PARIS' LEFT
A popular container plant in Victorian times, it still makes a good choice for growing in pots.

'SLATER'S CRIMSON CHINA' ABOVE
Once thought extinct, this genetically important rose has been rediscovered and again grows in gardens. Along with 'Old Blush' (see below), it arrived in Europe during the latter half of the 18th century and contributed its genes for recurrent bloom to the once-blooming European roses. Most modern red roses trace their origin to 'Slater's Crimson China', which, among other traits, passed on the white streak usually found on the outer petals of many modern red roses.

'ARCHDUKE CHARLES'
No two blooms in a cluster of this rose, named for the father of Emperor Franz Joseph, look alike.

'EUGENE DE BEAUHARNAIS'
Named for Prince Eugene, the brother of Napoleon's Empress Josephine.

'LOUIS PHILLIPE'
This rose was introduced during the reign of Louis Phillipe, the "Citizen King" of France.

'OLD BLUSH'
Said to be Thomas Moore's "last rose of summer." Along with 'Slater's Crimson China' (see above), this rose played a very important role in the development of modern roses by introducing and reinforcing the trait of recurrent bloom.

HYBRID GALLICA

As was the case with the damasks (see page 34), gallicas enjoyed an immense popularity during the Roman Empire. This class is especially noteworthy, not only because of its antiquity but also because it played a role in the lineage of other rose classes. Gallica blooms, which often retain their spicy fragrance after the petals have dried, are produced singly or in small clusters and sometimes in great abundance. They are small to medium-sized, and most are semidouble to very double Their vividly spotted and striped color patterns (see 'Camaieux' on page 45, for example) earned for some the epithet of "mad gallica," arising from the notion that their irregular color patterns reflected a kind of mental instability. Gallicas are nonrecurrent bloomers and are among the hardiest of old garden roses. The bushes are short and spread readily by producing suckers, and their canes are usually covered with fine prickles.

'CHARLES DE MILLS' ABOVE AND OPPOSITE
The petals have the feel of velvet, and no, no one comes along after the buds start to open and slices off the tops of the flowers. Few other old garden roses display this incredibly full and flat form. It may sometimes be called "Bizarre Triomphant."

'COMPLICATA'
Its name refers the fold or pleat in each petal. The plant grows unusually large for a gallica, making it a good choice for training it onto and through a large shrub.

LEFT TO RIGHT, TOP TO BOTTOM

'ALAIN BLANCHARD' ABOVE
Here is one of the "mad" gallicas, so named on account
of its "insane" color changes and spotting.

'ROSE DU MAÎTRE D'ÉCOLE'
Surprisingly, this is named after a village near Angers,
France, not for a schoolmaster.

'CAMAIEUX'
The name refers to "en camaieu" fabrics, which have
motifs in a single color on a coordinating or contrasting
background. Another "mad" gallica.

'BELLE ISIS'
Named for the Egyptian goddess of love, wisdom, and
beauty. It is a parent of 'Constance Spry', the first of
David Austin's English roses (see page 136).

'TUSCANY'
Scholars believe this is probably the 'Velvet Rose'
described by renowned herbalist John Gerard in his
Herball of 1596.

'CARDINAL DE RICHELIEU'
Cardinal Richelieu was minister to Louis XIII for 18
years. One of the most floriferous gallicas, its leaves
can be nearly hidden under a blanket of flowers in
luxurious shades of purple.

'LA BELLE SULTANE'
This beauty has a few too many petals to be called
a single-flowered rose.

'SUPERB TUSCAN' LEFT TOP
A rather old rose, predating 1837, it is sometimes confused with 'Tuscany' (see page 44), which has fewer petals.

'TRICOLORE DE FLANDRE' LEFT BOTTOM
The name is a salute to the flag of the medieval country of Flanders.

'ALIKA' ABOVE
The flowers on this very cold-hardy rose range from single to double, an unusual characteristic for any rose, old or modern.

'DUC DE GUICHE' RIGHT
The French de Guiche family includes many politicians and diplomats.

HYBRID MULTIFLORA

Members of this class are the descendants of crosses between *Rosa multiflora*, an Oriental species, and other rose classes, including damask, gallica, hybrid perpetual, and noisette. These roses produce single to double, typically fragrant and small blooms in large clusters that put forth a floriferous, fragrant display during the early weeks of summer, after which they produce the canes, sometimes reaching a length of 25ft (7.6m) that will bloom the following year. Depending upon the variety, they may be thorny or nearly thornless. The hybrid multifloras are very hardy and easy to grow. Some of the hybrids, as well as the parent species *Rosa multiflora*, have been used extensively for several decades as understock for grafting.

'RUSSELLIANA' ABOVE
Its scent, reminiscent of that found in damask roses, is unusual for this class.

'CHEVY CHASE'
Named not for the man but for the Maryland hometown of its breeder, Neils Hansen, this is one of the more popular members of its class.

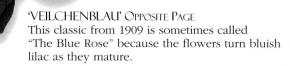

'VEILCHENBLAU' OPPOSITE PAGE
This classic from 1909 is sometimes called "The Blue Rose" because the flowers turn bluish lilac as they mature.

HYBRID PERPETUAL

The class name is a misnomer: these roses do not bloom perpetually but instead are remontant; that is, they bloom heavily during their first bloom cycle, followed by sparse production during the rest of the season. This class emerged during the early 1800s, when repeat-blooming bourbons and portlands and several other rose classes were crossed. Hybrid perpetuals enjoyed great popularity until the early 1900s, by which time there were approximately 2,800 varieties. A few 20th-century hybrid perpetuals produce blooms that possess hybrid tea form; indeed, the hybrid teas arose from crosses between hybrid perpetual and tea roses. The cold-hardy bushes typically grow to 6 feet, and some varieties have sported into climbers.

'BARONNE PRÉVOST'
One of the first hybrid perpetuals introduced into commerce, the Baronne produces gigantic, petal-packed flowers.

'MRS JOHN LAING' OPPOSITE PAGE
A vigorous grower even in poor soil, the unusual lilac-pink coloration of this rose sets it apart from most of the rest of the field.

'ROGER LAMBELIN'
The unique white edges and unusual petal shape make this rose stand out. This is a rose that responds well to (some say requires) more than the usual amount of care.

LEFT TO RIGHT, TOP TO BOTTOM

'FERDINAND PICHARD' ABOVE
One of the last hybrid perpetuals introduced (in 1921),
some argue it is more correctly considered a bourbon
(see page 28).

'AMERICAN BEAUTY'
The nonclimbing version became best known in the
cut-flower industry. Note how the deep pink color and
flower form differ from the usual depiction and
perception of this rose with a very famous name.

'BARONESS ROTHSCHILD'
The color gradations recall the color patterns of some
hybrid china roses (see page 38). Its petals have a soft,
silky texture.

'ENFANT DE FRANCE'
In comparison with 'Baroness Rothschild', the pink
petals of this rose have a velvety texture.

'ANNA DE DIESBACH'
This densely petaled confection was dedicated to the
daughter of Countess Diesbach of Switzerland.

'GÉNÉRAL JACQUEMINOT'
Named for a lesser general in French history, here is a
cornerstone of rose breeding: many of today's red roses
have this rose somewhere in their family trees.

'MABEL MORRISON'
Grayish green foliage hides numerous prickles on
the canes of this refreshing white sport of
'Baroness Rothschild' (see above).

LEFT TO RIGHT, TOP TO BOTTOM

'ULRICH BRÜNNER FILS' ABOVE
"Fils" means "son" in French. Ülrich Brunner,
the son, was a rosarian in Lausanne, Switzerland.

'MARCHESA BOCCELLA'
Its petals are smaller but more numerous than those of
other hybrid perpetuals. The plant tends to grow smaller
and more compact than others of its class.

'LA REINE'
The name means "The Queen." Registration records list
the petal count at 78.

'FRAU KARL DRUSCHKI'
Although introduced in 1901, this is still considered one of
the best white roses. Give the Frau plenty of room to
spread her arching canes.

'WALDFEE'
An extremely late (1960) addition to the hybrid perpetuals,
its name means "wood fairy." Here is one of the only few-
petaled roses in a class famous for its double flowers.

'PAUL NEYRON'
Easily capable of producing flowers that measure eight
inches in diameter, the growth habit of this variety
is similarly superlative.

'SYDONIE'
Its flat, quartered blooms (its petals are arranged in
distinct, often four, groups) produce a fragrance much
like that of the damasks (see page 34).

MOSS

Although documented records on the precise origin of these roses are lacking, moss roses are believed to have arisen as sports (mutations) from the centifolias (see page 32) and the damasks (see page 34). The sports displayed the novel characteristic of soft or prickly glandular growths on their sepals and peduncles that resulted in the mossy appearance that gives the class its name. Moss roses enjoyed their greatest popularity between the late 18th and late 19th centuries. Attempts by hybridizers of that period to develop recurrent blooming moss roses were essentially unsuccessful, since the repeat-blooming creations had little moss. The nonclimbing varieties are bushy and usually moderately tall, although some are short enough to be included in small gardens.

'ALFRED DE DALMAS'
A compact bush, normally growing to 3ft (1m) at the most. Unlike most moss roses, 'Alfred de Dalmas' produces repeat blooms rather dependably.

'COMMUNIS' OPPOSITE PAGE
Sometimes called "Common Moss" because it has been grown in many gardens for hundreds of years.

'CRESTED MOSS'
The very elaborate moss suggested this rose's official name as well as one of its synonyms, "Chapeau de Napoleon" ("Napoleon's Hat"): quite frequently the moss is arranged triangularly, like a three-cornered hat.

'COMMUNIS'
The pine-scented moss and rose-scented petals combine into a fragrant combination that is anything but common. Also see the large picture to the far right.

LEFT TO RIGHT, TOP TO BOTTOM

'NUITS DE YOUNG' ABOVE
The relatively small 1 1/2in (4cm) blooms appear in
shades of purplish black, a color not often found
among moss roses.

'DEUIL DE PAUL FONTAINE'
Its name essentially means "mourning for Paul
Fontaine," the introducer of this rose. It is one of the
few moss roses that blooms more than once a season.

'GÉNÉRAL KLÉBER'
The man was one of Napoleon's commanders
during the campaign against Egypt. The rose is
abundantly mossed.

'MME DE LA ROCHE-LAMBERT'
The extensive moss makes the canes of this rose seen
almost thornless. Treat this rose well, and you will be
rewarded with some blooms beyond the normal season.

'GLOIRE DES MOUSSEUSES'
Its elegantly arranged 4 in (1 1/2cm) blooms explain
the translation of its name, "glory of the mosses."

'OLD RED MOSS'
The original name and date of introduction are not
known for this supposedly very old rose.

'COMTESSE DE MURINAIS'
One of the tallest of the moss roses, this vigorous
grower can easily reach 6ft (1.8m). Its moss is
unusually hard to the touch, adding to the sensory
delight this rose provides.

NOISETTE

The origin of this class is traceable to a cross between the repeat-blooming china rose 'Old Blush' (see page 40) with the white *Rosa moschata*. There is some debate as to whether the cross was an accident of nature or a deliberate cross made by John Champneys of North Carolina. In any event, the result was the rose 'Champneys' Pink Cluster' (see below), which is found in the lineage of much of this class. Most noisettes are gracefully climbing plants that produce small to large-sized clusters of fragrant blooms in shades of white, pink, and yellow. The plants grow best in warmer climates, although some will tolerate colder climates if given enough winter protection.

'NASTARANA'
This geographical form of *Rosa moschata* is said to have come from Persia (present-day Iran) in 1879.

'LAMARQUE' OPPOSITE PAGE
Introduced by an amateur hybridizer, this vigorous rose produces strongly fragrant flowers, which, like some others in its class, nod attractively.

'CHAMPNEY'S PINK CLUSTER'
This rose, the first of its class, bears large clusters of blooms that recall the color and fragrance of it parents (see the introductory paragraph).

LEFT TO RIGHT, TOP TO BOTTOM

'JAUNE DESPREZ' ABOVE
Once considered one of the most fragrant roses,
its perfume still enthralls its admirers.

'AIMÉE VIBERT'
Named for its French hybridizer's daughter, this rose's
synonym, "Nivea," evokes the beauty of new-fallen snow.

'MARÉCHAL NIEL'
Napoleon III's minister of war is remembered here.
In great demand at the zenith of its popularity and
commercially profitable for florists, this golden beauty
is still treasured by many devotees of old garden roses.

'MME ALFRED CARRIÈRE'
Voted "best white climber" by England's Royal National
Rose Society in 1908, this rose can show a heavy overlay
of pink under favorable conditions.

'RÊVE D'OR'
French for "golden dream," it features delicate touches
of peach in its reverie.

'ALISTER STELLA GRAY'
The memory of a relative of the hybridizer Alexander Hill
Gray lives on through this pastel creation.

'CÉLINE FORESTIER'
The hybridizer Trouillard named this rose for one of
his close friends.

PORTLAND

The name of this class is derived from a late 18th century rose that was named for the second Duchess of Portland. The original repeat-blooming portland rose is believed to have been produced by crossing 'Autumn Damask' (see page 36) with the species 'Apothecary's Rose' (see page 10). French hybridizers quickly recognized the importance of the portland's repeat-bloom habit and embarked on a hybridizing program that yielded numerous multipetaled, fragrant, relatively cold-hardy varieties. Unfortunately, only a small number of portlands survived beyond their peak period of popularity in the 1840s, when their quality of repeat-flowering captured the interest of many contemporary rosarians. Blooms are nestled atop a short peduncle (bloomstalk), which makes them appear to wear a collar of foliage just below the base of the bloom. The bushes are usually small and compact, making them ideal for small gardens, but the canes are frequently thorny.

ROSE DU ROI
The rose featured prominently in the creation of the hybrid perpetuals (see page 50).

MME KNORR OPPOSITE PAGE
A strongly fragrant rose with a mysterious past: its parentage is unknown.

'COMTE DE CHAMBORD'
The name memorializes the grandson of Charles X. He died in exile after refusing the French crown.

'ARTHUR DE SANSAL'
Named for the noted European horticulturist who expended a great deal of effort breeding roses.

TEA

One of the first tea roses to arrive in Europe during the 19th century was the pink 'Hume's Tea-scented China'. It and other roses from China were frequently transported on ships that carried tea leaves to Europe. Hybridizers quickly recognized the importance of tea roses' recurrent bloom capabilities, along with their then-rare yellow bloom color. In time, the teas gave rise to the now hugely popular hybrid teas (see page 104). Tea blooms are mildly fragrant, occur in small clusters in a wide range of colors, and frequently droop or nod, due to weak peduncles. Some display the high-centered flower form so common in their hybrid tea descendants (see 'Maman Cochet', page 69). The teas have a wide range of growth habit, making them suitable for every garden. The plants are notably cold tender and produce usually slender canes bearing coarsely toothed leaves.

'MME LOMBARD'
Sometimes called the "cemetery rose" because it is often found growing in graveyards.

'SOMBREUIL' OPPOSITE PAGE
Named for Mlle de Sombreuil, a heroine in the French Revolution. The color can vary from pure white to cream, with hints of warm tan or even pink.

'LADY HILLINGDON'
A strong tea fragrance graces the blossoms of this plant, which is nearly as cold hardy as a hybrid tea.

LEFT TO RIGHT, TOP TO BOTTOM

'ROSETTE DELIZY' ABOVE
Resembling the color variations found in the flowers
of some hybrid china roses, this tea displays a
kaleidoscope of colors among its many petals.
Its fragrance is reminiscent of tropical fruit punch.

'FRANCIS DEBREUIL'
The name honors the grandfather of Francis Meilland,
noted French hybridizer and member of the dynastic
House of Meilland. The Meillands have given the
gardening world many famous roses, including 'Peace'
(see pages 79 and 108) and the 'Meidiland' series .

'MAMAN COCHET'
Suitable for growing in a container, left unpruned this
plant can grow to 7ft (2.2m). The flower form closely
resembles that of hybrid teas, the class that was
developed from the teas (see page 104). The surname
Cochet recalls an important French hybridizing family.

'MRS B. R. CANT'
This rose can bloom well into winter in warm areas.

'MRS DUDLEY CROSS'
Unfortunately, production of these enormous blooms
is sometimes stingy.

'MONS TILLIER'
Like many of the teas, the Monsieur prefers warmer
climates or the shelter of a greenhouse to grow best.

'PERLE DES JARDINS'
The pearl of the garden is, ironically, raised primarily in
greenhouses, because it does not tolerate weather well.

AYRSHIRE

At its zenith during the first half of the 19th century, this class is now represented by a group of no more than approximately 20 varieties. They are considered to be hybrids of *Rosa arvensis*, which was used in crosses with other old garden roses such as chinas, teas, and noisettes. It is believed that the Earl of London in Ayrshire, for whom this class is named, was responsible for developing this class. Ayrshires are robust growers with a rambling habit and are suited to colder climates. Their nonrecurrent, semidouble or double blooms are produced singly or in small clusters and are most frequently white; however, dark red, pink, or mauve blooms may also be found within the class. Some varieties produce a perfume that has been described as myrrhlike, similar to that found in some of the modern "English" roses (see page 134).

BOURSALT

Many of the varieties in this class were the creations of the French botanist Henri Boursalt, for whom the class is named. Only a few of the approximately 50 varieties are known today. Their small to large semidouble to double blooms, sometimes striped with pink, red, or mauve, are nonrecurrent and are borne in clusters. The leaves are deeply toothed and may turn reddish orange in autumn. The boursalts typically have a climbing or rambling growth habit. The canes are smooth or may have a few prickles and sometimes have a reddish cast.

'MME DE SANCY DE PARABÈRE'
Here is one of only two boursalts known in cultivation today. The arrangement of large petals surrounding smaller ones is known as an "anemone center."

70

HYBRID BRACTEATA

This class consists of fewer than ten varieties, some of which are apparently no longer in cultivation. Typically, the nonrecurrent white or light pink blooms are large and double. One notable exception is the highly popular 'Mermaid', which not only is a repeat bloomer but also produces single, creamy yellow flowers (see left). The hybrid bracteatas have a climbing or rambling growth habit that can achieve heights up to 30 ft (9m), especially in warm climates, where it may be locally common to see 'Mermaid' gracing homes and gardens.

'MERMAID'
This variety spreads quickly and can grow rapidly to 30 feet in favorable regions. Some people prize 'Mermaid' more for its intricately gorgeous stamens than for its flower color.

HYBRID EGLANTERIA

Roses in this class are frequently referred to as sweet briars, referring to their apple-scented foliage and hooked prickles ("thorns"). The complete parentage of most varieties is unknown; the species *Rosa eglanteria* may have been crossed with a bourbon or a hybrid perpetual to produce some of the varieties. Blooms are frequently five-petaled and produced in large clusters; some varieties produce semidouble or double blooms that are usually small. With rare exceptions, blooms are nonrecurrent and are borne on robust and hardy bushes.

'LADY PENZANCE'
One of a large group of roses bred by Lord Penzance in the late 1800s.

HYBRID FOETIDA

Almost half of the approximately 40 members of this class produce blooms in some shade or blend of yellow. The frequent occurrence of yellow reflects the species ancestors of these hybrids that played a significant role in introducing yellow into the gene pool of many old and modern roses. Blooms are scented, semidouble or double, and usually occur once per season. The hardy bushes have a loose, rather than dense, growth habit and are typically 4 to 5ft (1.2 to 1.5m) tall. Some varieties make suitable climbers.

'SOLEIL D'OR' ABOVE
This rarely encountered citrus-scented beauty is found in the parentage of many modern yellow roses.

'HARISON'S YELLOW' OPPOSITE
Naturalized across the United States by early settlers, this is claimed by some to be the famed "Yellow Rose of Texas." It began its long history in the garden of New York City attorney George F. Harison.

HYBRID SEMPERVIRENS

During Victorian times, this class of roses was often referred to as the "Evergreen Roses," a designation that alluded to the near evergreen nature of their glossy foliage. The French names for several varieties that are still available today hint that they came about through the efforts of French hybridizers during the first half of the 19th century. Although bloom production for most varieties is nonrecurrent, there are a few that will provide a second light flush of bloom in the autumn. Their vigorous, climbing growth habit may reach 15ft (4.5m) or more in some varieties and, as a group, they are usually not the earliest roses to bloom in the spring.

'FÉLICITÉ ET PERPÉTUE'
Named by the hybridizer for his twin daughters, who were named for the Christian martyrs who died together in the year 203.

HYBRID SETIGERA

Although definitely not one of the largest classes of rose, the hybrid setigeras have something to offer every gardener. A few varieties display a short, compact growth habit, but most are vigorous climbers that thrive even when neglected, a trait they inherited from their *Rosa setigera* parent, a species native to North America and commonly known as the prairie rose (also see page 20). Their fragrant blooms are large, usually cupped, and produced in large clusters. Bloom colors in this class are mostly shades of pink and red, but there are a few varieties that produce white, yellow, mauve, and striped flowers. A special feature of the hybrid setigeras is the appearance of their blooms, which occurs when most other roses have completed their first bloom, thus filling a void left by fellow roses.

'FRÜHLINGSGOLD'
Wilhelm Kordes created a series of roses using *Rosa spinosissima*. All of their names begin with the prefix 'Fruhling-', which means "spring" in German.

'STANWELL PERPETUAL' OPPOSITE PAGE
Found as a seedling in a garden in Stanwell in Essex, England, this rose has gone on to achieve great popularity on account of its vigor and recurrent bloom.

HYBRID SPINOSISSIMA

Members of this class are popularly known as Scotch roses or Burnet roses. They are very disease resistant and tolerant of neglect. Their bushy growth of slender and gracefully arching canes is noted for the dense covering of prickles. Bushes are usually large and well suited for use as a natural barrier, while a few varieties are short and suitable for small gardens. Foliage is characteristically small and nearly fernlike. The spinosissimas were initially hybridized in the early 1800s and are nonrecurrent bloomers, with the exception of 'Stanwell Perpetual'.

MISCELLANEOUS OLD GARDEN ROSES

'FORTUNE'S DOUBLE YELLOW'
Discovered by famous plant explorer Robert Fortune in a Chinese garden during the early 19th century.

As is often the case in any system of plant or animal classification, there are a few individuals that do not seem to fit into any of the existing categories of classification. Such is the case of a few old garden roses whose growth characteristics or pedigree have prompted their placement in this catchall class. These roses are most often encountered as long-time residents of public or private gardens. For the most part, varieties placed in this class are nonrecurrent.

EMPRESS JOSEPHINE & PIERRE-JOSEPH REDOUTÉ

Perhaps the most famous of all rose patrons was France's Empress Josephine. The wife of Napoleon Bonaparte, Josephine selected Malmaison, an estate six and one-half miles southwest of Paris, as a retreat for herself and her power-seeking mate. The run-down chateau was surrounded by poorly maintained grounds, but with a visionary eye Josephine is reported to have paid 300,000F for the estate, investing an additional 600,000F for its transformation. Although the renovation and furnishing of the house were impressive, it is the gardens of Malmaison that of are of great-est interest to gardeners. Because a horticulturist accompanied Napoleon on all of his expeditions, many new and unusual plants found their way to the gardens at Malmaison. Additional specimens were supplied by ambassadors and foreign dignitaries who knew of Josephine's love for plants and especially roses. Unfortunately, all did not remain well with the couple. Napoleon wanted an heir, so in 1808 the childless Josephine found herself cast aside for a younger wife of childbearing age. She received Malmaison in the divorce settlement, and sympathetic friends, associates,

and dignitaries from around the globe showered Josephine with rose plants so she might continue to pursue her dream of a garden featuring all the roses of the world. A team of workers cared for the gardens, catalogued the plants, and even depicted them in detailed artworks. This latter task fell to Pierre-Joseph Redouté. Instructed to make his illustrations esthetically pleasing and botanically correct, Redouté was commissioned to record all of the roses of Malmaison. At the time of Josephine's death in 1814, Redouté had completed 169 of the 260 roses on the estate. Soon afterward, Redouté began working with Claude-Antonine Thory, a botanist also under Josephine's sponsorship, to produce *Les Roses*. This 30-part publication contained prints and descriptions of all 169 roses Redouté had depicted. Because no other records have ever been found, these illustrations are the only accurate record of Josephine's roses that grew at Malmaison. Redouté's work is widely considered as a benchmark of botanical drawing. Unfortunately, the originals were destroyed in a fire in the library of the Louvre.

'EMPRESS JOSEPHINE' OPPOSITE PAGE
Its veined petals are almost translucent. Named for the most famous of rose patrons (see above).

MODERN ROSES

For more than a century, hybrid teas (the most easily recognized of all the roses classed as "modern,") have been considered the benchmark by which most other flowers are judged. Their classic high-centered buds borne on long stems are perfect for cutting and arranging, and the floral trade certainly makes extensive use of these attributes. No wedding or commemorative event – not to mention Valentine's Day – is considered complete without the inclusion of at least a few of these. The 1867 introduction of 'La France' (see page 104) is recognized as the beginning of the hybrid tea class. Soon after 'La France' appeared, the gates swung wide as hybridizers continued to develop the class and introduce new varieties in an ever-increasing kaleidoscope of colors and combinations. The bright or iridescent hues missing from old garden roses – the oranges and bright yellows, the apricots and ambers, clear reds, and many other colors never before seen in roses – were enthusiastically welcomed by gardeners everywhere. (See pages 104 – 113 for a sampling of the colors in which hybrid teas are available today.)

Additional forays into hybridization resulted in many useful rose classes. Chief among these were the hybrid musks, a very fragrant and cluster-flowered class useful on pergolas, fences, and other supports (see page 96), and the polyanthas, a forerunner of the floribunda class with many of the same characteristics (see page 80). Polyanthas never quite attained the popularity they so richly deserved because they were upstaged, rather quickly, by the emerging and more diverse floribundas. This class provides a veritable bouquet of flowers on one bush, and it somewhat mimics the old garden roses in that the blooms come in all shapes and sizes. They, too, offer a color range any gardener could possibly want, and many are fragrant as well. They can often be grown in containers, so they can be enjoyed by anyone lacking ground space.
All that is said of floribundas can also be claimed by another modern rose – the miniature – a class that has many uses in the landscape and is a boon for those with limited space. Great progress has been made in recent years to expand the color range and garden desirability of the minis (see page 122).

'DORTMUND'
(Hybrid Kordesii)
The hybrid kordesiis are a small but useful group of sturdy plants.
See page 94.

The quest never ends to perfect the rose, and, to this end, a marriage of sorts has resulted in a group of roses commonly referred to as "English roses" (see page 134 for a sampling of these roses). Their rather complex parentage has resulted in a tipping of the hat to romantic appearance of the old garden roses while incorporating the good qualities (such as repeat bloom and more compact growth) of modern roses. In addition to David Austin, other hybridizers have answered the call by producing similar modern shrubs marketed under recognizable group names, such as Meilland's Romantica series. This group has many of the soft colors so often found in old garden roses as well as their full-petaled or "cabbagey" blooms. Their fragrance is generally pronounced and reminiscent of many of the old garden roses, but their color range is much wider.

'CARIBBEAN'
(Grandiflora)
Grandifloras combine characteristics of their parents, the hybrid teas and floribundas. See page 88.

A BRIEF HISTORY OF 'PEACE'

In the summer of 1935, 23-year-old rose hybridizer Francis Meilland was at work at his family's nursery in southern France. Detailed records indicate the 55 flowers pollinated that day resulted in 800 seedlings, 50 of which were selected for further trial and observation. One of those roses, #3-35-40, became 'Peace' – perhaps the most widely recognized and grown rose of all time. By the summer of 1939, the plant still known as #3-35-40 was gaining attention. A decision to market the rose was made, and bud eyes (propagation material) were shipped to the Conard-Pyle Company in the United States as well as to nurseries in Germany and Italy. A a result of the outbreak of World War II in September, communication within the rose industry became very difficult, so it is little surprise that #3-35-40 was introduced under several different names. In Germany it was called 'Gloria Dei' and in Italy, 'Gioia'. In France, the Meillands named the rose 'Mme A. Meilland' in memory of Francis' mother, who had died a few years previously. The end of World War II, in 1945, provided the inspiration for 'Peace' as the rose's name in the US market, and its selection as the floral emblem of the newly formed United Nations later that year virtually ensured the former #3-35-40's place in history.

But sentimentality is not this rose's only claim to fame. Perfectly symmetrical, 6in (15cm) blooms in varying hues of yellow and pink atop long, sturdy stems make it a favorite in the garden and for exhibition. 'Peace' is a hardy, free-flowering rose that has proven itself as a pollen and seed parent of approximately 300 offspring, including 18 sports. More than five decades after its introduction, it continues to be a consistent seller that experienced rose lovers and novice gardeners all know to ask for by name. (See page 108)

'PARTY GIRL'
(Miniature)
Miniature roses have become enormously popular in recent years. See page 122.

Modern roses include a wide variety of classes, so there is something for everyone. Whether the need is for a climber, a container plant, a cutting garden, or a border, there is a modern rose for every need. As hybridizers continue to expand the rose world, it is somewhat gratifying to see the rose coming full circle to meet the needs of modern gardeners. What was good in the old is being given more attention in the new, including resistance to disease, inclusion of fragrance, and attention to the needs of the landscape and the environment. This blending of the old with the new can result only in a growing desire for the rose and the ability for everyone to grow and enjoy the ultimate flower.

SEPARATING THE OLD FROM THE NEW

What differentiates modern roses from their old garden rose counterparts? Although one might think of flower size, growth habit, or even bloom frequency as determining factors, it is actually the 1867 introduction of 'La France' by French hybridizer Jean Guillot that marks the creation of the hybrid tea class and provides the "magic" date delineating which roses are considered modern as compared to those recognized as old garden roses. This is not to say that all roses introduced after 1867 are modern roses. The key to this puzzle lies in the date a given roses class was officially recognized. For example, the hybrid perpetual 'Waldfee' was introduced into commerce in 1960, but because the hybrid perpetual class was established prior to 1867, this rose is considered an old garden rose, even though it was introduced nearly a century after the year that divides the old from the new.

'SEXY REXY'
(Floribunda)
Many floribundas bloom with great abandon, making them excellent choices for beds and borders. See page 80.

FLORIBUNDA

As the class name seems to imply, floribundas produce flowers in abundance. Their best displays are in late spring and early summer, but they will normally produce additional small flushes (periods of bloom) later in the year. Their stature is bushier and usually much smaller than the hybrid teas (see page 104), and they bear their flowers primarily in clusters. Most floribunda blooms are of the decorative, casual, or single-petaled style, although some have the classic high-centered hybrid tea form. A wide array of colors is available, with striping (such as that shown by 'Scentimental' and 'Purple Tiger'; please turn the page) becoming increasingly popular in recent years. The fragrance in floribundas is usually light and fruity. These plants can be successfully used in mass plantings or as a short hedge.

'OLD MASTER'
This intricately colored offering is one of hybridizer Sam McGredy's first "hand-painted" roses.

'GINGERNUT' OPPOSITE PAGE
Its lively color plus a light, spicy scent make its name perfect for this rose.

'SHEILA'S PERFUME'
Sheila is the wife of the hybridizer John Sheridan.

'INVINCIBLE'
This striking dark red floribunda is from the Dutch hybridizer de Ruiter.

LEFT TO RIGHT, TOP TO BOTTOM

'ICEBERG'
One of the best white roses, it also occurs in a climbing variety (see page 86) that can grace a wall or trellis.

'FRENCH LACE'
Sometimes nearly white, this variety makes an excellent cut flower.

'SUMMER FASHION'
The edges of its petals spread as the bloom ages.

'LADY OF THE DAWN'
Sometimes there are so many flowers that its stems have difficulty supporting the blooms.

'FRAGRANT APRICOT'
A strong damask/musk scent and hybrid tea flower form make this floribunda a standout. Also see the title page.

'SWEET DREAM'
It recalls the quartered flower form of old garden roses.

'ENGLISH MISS'
Named by its English hybridizer for his three-year-old daughter. Purplish foliage nicely complements the blooms.

'HANNAH GORDON'
This unforgettable creation bears the name of a popular British actress who loves roses.

'BLUEBERRY HILL'
The bright yellow stamens contrast beautifuly with the unusual mauve color of the petals.

'SUNSPRITE'
Winner of the Gamble Fragrance Award in 1979.

'FELLOWSHIP'
The color makes you want to be in its company.

'SCENTIMENTAL'
Fragrance, old-fashioned form, and vivid coloring all come together in one memorable rose.

'PURPLE TIGER'
Its striking purple color is further enhanced with striping and spotting that changes from one flower to the next.

'CHINATOWN'
This very fragrant rose has a peachy scent.

'EYEPAINT'
The nickname – adopted by the hybridizer after he first saw this eyecatching rose – stuck.

'KANEGEM'
Boasting a remarkably high-centered exhibition flower form, 'Kanegem' tolerates both hot and cold climates.

LEFT TO RIGHT, TOP TO BOTTOM

'EUROPEANA'
The plants bloom so profusely that the canes sometimes cannot support the weight of the flower clusters. This rose, introduced in the 1960s, has won several major awards and remains popular in American gardens.

'PLAYGIRL'
A surprisingly colored offspring of 'Playboy' (see below), its petal color is anything but shy.

'BILL WARRINER'
This was bred from 'Impatient' (see page 86) and the yellow 'Sunflare', two of hybridizer Bill Warriner's award-winning roses, and then named in his honor.

'TOOTSIE'
Disease-resistant foliage sets off this "hand-painted" rose.

'ESCAPADE'
Light pruning, instead of the more traditional heavy pruning, will allows this variety to take on the appearance of a shrub.

'BRASS BAND'
Named for its brassy-colored blooms, the coloration of this rose changes with time and local growing conditions.

'PLAYBOY'
Flamboyant color is its trademark and the source of its name. See above for its descendant 'Playgirl'.

'DICKY'
One of the most popular floribundas, 'Dicky' was renamed for the US market from the British 'Anisley Dickson', which honors the hybrizer's wife.

'PRISCILLA BURTON'
Named for the wife of a British gardening firm executive, the flower colors are never consistently the same, which is one hallmark of the McGredy "hand-painted" roses.

'DRUMMER BOY' RIGHT
This pulsatingly red rose makes a dramatic low display when used in mass plantings.

'FIRST EDITION' FAR RIGHT TOP
Known as 'Arnauld Delbard' in Europe to honor the hybridizer's grandson.

'ICEBERG, CLIMBING' FAR RIGHT BOTTOM
A sport of the justly famous 'Iceberg' (see page 82), this rose is excellent for softening the look of a new brick wall or to complement the coloring of a weathered wall.

'LAUGHTER LINES' EXTREME RIGHT TOP
It's not known for certain, but could the name have been suggested by the dark pink lines on its petals?

'IMPATIENT' EXTREME RIGHT BOTTOM
Numerous prickles cover the stems of this rose with insistently colored flowers.

GRANDIFLORA

The offspring of crosses between hybrid teas (see page 104) and floribundas (see page 80), grandifloras are similar to hybrid teas in many ways, with two major exceptions: grandiflora bushes tend to grow much taller than their hybrid tea counterparts, and grandifloras produce their blooms in clusters more readily than hybrid teas, a trait they inheirited from their floribunda parents. From the floribundas they also acquired slightly greater cold hardiness and near-continuous bloom. The flower form of grandifloras is similar to the hybrid teas: usually double, in solid shades of white, red, pink, yellow, and orange as well as blends and dramatic bicolors. Because of their size, the grandifloras must be given sufficient space in the garden and should be located behind lower-growing varieties. The first grandiflora, 'Queen Elizabeth' (see page 90), was introduced by Walter Lammerts in 1954. It is a cross between his hybrid tea 'Charlotte Armstrong' and the floribunda 'Floradora'.

'HEART O' GOLD'
Golden petals nestling in the center suggested the name. The coloration brings to mind the combinations found in some of the tea roses (see 'Rosette Delizy', page 68).

'REBA MCENTIRE' OPPOSITE PAGE
This glowing beauty was named for the popular country/western singer through a "name that rose" contest.

'REJOICE'
The hybridizer must have rejoiced when this variety won the first Gold Medal awarded at the American Rose Society trial grounds in Shreveport, Louisiana in 1985.

LEFT TO RIGHT, TOP TO BOTTOM

'AQUARIUS'
Named for the zodiacal sign and the astrological age.

'SWEET SUCCESS'
Its exquisite from can bring success on the show bench.

'QUEEN ELIZABETH'
The first to be classed as a grandiflora, this rose has won
many top awards throughout the world.
See the introduction on page 88.

'PRIMA DONNA'
Bred in Japan. Some feel 'Prima Donna' is better suited for
growing in a greenhouse than outdoors in the garden.

'CLASSIE LASSIE'
A strong fragrance complements its coloration.

'MAGIC LANTERN'
This sport of 'Gold Medal' (see below) was enjoyed in
Europe for several years before it reached the US.

'ARIZONA'
Its colors are reminiscent of an Arizona sunset.

'CARIBBEAN'
The warm shades of this award-winning rose reflect the
ambience of its namesake region of the world.

'WAIHEKE'
It bears one of several Maori-based names used by
hybridizer Sam McGredy of New Zealand.

'GOLD MEDAL'
Some describe its fragrance as tealike, while others
consider it fruity.

'SHINING HOUR'
Hybridizer Bill Warriner (see page 84 for a namesake)
crossed two of his previous yellow creations to produce
this rose.

'FAME!'
It has a long vase life as a cut flower.

'SHREVEPORT'
The name honors the Louisiana home city of the
headquarters of the American Rose Society.

'QUAKER STAR'
Named to mark the tercentenary of the death of George
Fox, founder of the Quaker movement.

'SCARLET KNIGHT'
Its blackish red buds open into large blooms.

'LOVE'
Here is one of the trio that includes 'Honor' and 'Cherish',
all introduced by hybridizer Bill Warriner in 1980.

THE TOURNAMENT OF ROSES

In 1890, the midwinter blooming of flowers and trees bearing fruit inspired members of Pasadena, California's Valley Hunt Club to stage the first Tournament of Roses parade. Held on New Year's Day 1890, it boasted 2,000 attendees who watched the parade of flower-covered carriages. The abundance of flowers prompted Professor Charles F. Holder, a member of the Valley Hunt Club, to suggest "Tournament of Roses" as an appropriate name for the festival, of which the parade was a part.

In the years following, the festival expanded to include marching bands and motorized floats. Games held on the town lot included ostrich races, bronco-busting demonstrations, and a race between a camel and an elephant. Reviewing stands were built along the parade route, and Eastern newspapers began writing about the event. In 1895, the activities grew too large for the Valley Hunt Club to handle, and the Tournament of Roses Association took charge.

Every New Year's morning, nearly one million curb-side spectators crowd every available space along the parade route. Those lucky enough to garner a good position along the route are treated to an unforgettable two-hour display of magnificent floral floats, talented marching bands, and high-stepping equestrian units. Sharing in the festivities are an estimated 425 million television viewers in more than 100 countries, who enjoy not only the parade but also the Rose Bowl football game, the longest-standing tradition of any collegiate conference and bowl association.

The Rose Bowl game traces its history to 1902, when the Tournament of Roses Association chose to enhance the day's festivities by adding a football game. The first game was played between Stanford University and the University of Michigan, with Michigan winning 49-0, with Stanford bowing out in the third quarter. In the face of such a defeat, the Association dropped football in favor of Roman-style chariot races. In 1916, football returned to stay, and the crowds soon outgrew the stands in Tournament Park. The Association's 1920 president, William L. Leishman, envisioned a stadium similar to the Yale Bowl, the first great modern football stadium, and enlisted the help of architect Myron Hunt and builder William A. Taylor.

The original stadium, a 57,000-seat horseshoe-shaped arena, was dubbed the "Rose Bowl" by local newspaper Harlan "Dusty" Hall, who also served as press agent for the Tournament. On January 1, 1923, the Tournament held the first Rose Bowl game The stadium grew with the games popularity, so in 1928 its south end was filled in, increasing the seating capacity to 76,000. Capacity has continued to grow through the years to its current 91,000, although seating was found for a record crowd of 106,869 on January 1, 1973.

Though its fame is worldwide, the Tournament of Roses remains true to its hometown origins. In 1983, the Association created the Tournament of Roses Foundation, a non-profit corporation that makes annual grants to activities that enhance the traditions of the Tournament of Roses and to worthwhile programs that contribute to the civic, cultural, and educational advancement of the Pasadena area.

'TOURNAMENT OF ROSES'
This rose is a fitting tribute to a beloved event.

HYBRID KORDESII

The rose class, which includes *Rosa* x *kordesii* and its hybrids, is composed of some of the hardiest and most disease-resistant modern roses. *Rosa* x *kordesii*, introduced in 1941 by Wilhelm Kordes of Germany, is a seedling of 'Max Graf', which is the offspring of *Rosa rugosa* and *Rosa wichurana*. The hybrid kordesiis are cluster-flowering, usually in tones of pink and red. They are recurrent bloomers and produce large hips when not deadheaded. The plants are large and vigorous, and many will climb.

'WILLIAM BAFFIN' ABOVE
This hybrid kordesii is named for one of the explorers who searched for the Northwest Passage.

'SYMPATHIE' OPPOSITE PAGE
Another hybrid kordesii, 'Sympathie' produces masses of deep red, very fragrant flowers on vigorous plants that can grow to 12ft (3.6m) or even more.

'GERANIUM'
This form of *Rosa moyesii* bears a profusion of very showy orange hips on its rather delicate canes in autumn.

HYBRID MOYESII

Rosa moyesii and its descendants, with their unique bottle-shaped and colorful hips (fruit), provide one of the most striking autumn offerings of the genus *Rosa*. The single or semidouble blooms are borne intermittently over the entire season. Vigorous and hardy, the hybrids typically have an open growth habit, with long, sweeping canes that reach 8 to 10ft (2.5 to 3m) in length. Their foliage is dark green and often fernlike in its delicacy. The species was introduced into England from western and northern China in 1903, and the class is named after the Rev. E. J. Moyes.

HYBRID MUSK

The class of roses known today as the hybrid musks has a very complicated ancestry. Many members of this class have only a remote relation to the parent species, *Rosa moschata*, a large and vigorous grower native to southern Europe and western Asia. Its single white blooms are produced recurrently, are borne in clusters, and have a strong fragrance. *Rosa moschata*, when crossed with a member of the china group, produced one of the first members of the noisette class (see page 60). A subsequent cross between that noisette and *Rosa multiflora* produced 'Aglaia' and 'Trier', the prototypes of the hybrid musk class. These two roses, when further bred with various polyanthas, noisettes, teas, and even hybrid teas, resulted in the varieties now known as hybrid musks.

'CORNELIA'
This is one of the last of the hybrid musks introduced by Rev. Pemberton, a major hybridizer of this class.

'BALLERINA' OPPOSITE PAGE
Considered by many rosarians as one of the easiest roses to grow, and by many others as one of the easiest to enjoy.

'PROSPERITY'
Grows more upright than many other hybrid musks introduced by Rev. Pemberton (see 'Cornelia', above).

'BELINDA'
The cut-flower industry as embraced 'Belinda' as one of their own, raising it primarily in greenhouses.

LEFT TO RIGHT, TOP TO BOTTOM

'BUFF BEAUTY'
The widow of Rev. Pemberton's gardener introduced this rose to commerce 13 years after his death. Many gardeners are very glad she did.

'ERFURT'
Sharing the name of a town in central Germany, 'Erfurt' begins producing colorful hips (fruit) following its first flush of bloom and continues doing so throughout the growing season.

'DANAE'
Consider growing 'Danae' as an attractive hedge.

'BLOOMFIELD DAINTY'
Here is one of several roses hybridized by Captain Thomas. All of their names begin with 'Bloomfield'.

'PENELOPE'
Its vigorous habit can be tamed, but 'Penelope' is at its loveliest when only lightly pruned.

'NYMPHENBURG'
Wilhelm Kordes named this rose in tribute to the palace and gardens of Nymphenburg.

'MOONLIGHT'
One of Rev. Pemberton's first introductions, its wide-ranging habit makes 'Moonlight' useful as a climber.

HYBRID RUGOSA

Rosa rugosa and its hybrids are some of the most easily identified members of the genus Rosa, thanks to their rugose (heavily lined) foliage that gave the species its name. The species (see pages 16 and 20) and most of the hybrids have fragrant, recurrent-blooming flowers that are followed by large, red hips (fruit). The rugosas are one of the easiest groups of rose to grow, since they are very cold hardy and do not require a spray program to prevent fungal diseases. In fact, they will often be harmed by spraying.

'MARTIN FROBISHER'
This very cold-hardy rose shares a name with the 16th century English explorer who made three voyages to the Baffin Island area of Canada in search of the Northwest Passage.

'FRAU DAGMAR HARTOPP' OPPOSITE PAGE
The Frau is especially beautiful later in the growing season, when the clove-scented pink blooms and orange-red hips appear simultaneously. Viewed by many as one of the most satisfying of all roses.

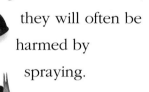

'PINK GROOTENDORST'
Several hybrid rugosas produce clustered, carnation-like small blooms, including the medium red 'F. J. Grootendorst', from which this rose sported, and the light pink 'Fimbriata'.

'LINDA CAMPBELL'
Linda Campbell was a noted American Rose society member, writer, and author who died at a young age.

LEFT TO RIGHT, TOP TO BOTTOM

'JENS MUNK' ABOVE
Cooler weather brings out the best in this rose from the
Canada Department of Agriculture.

'STAR DELIGHT'
This unusual hybrid rugosa was bred by Ralph Moore,
a hybridizer most noted for his work in producing
outstanding miniature roses.

'HENRY HUDSON'
A product of Canadian research, it is named for the
explorer of Hudson Bay fame who died seeking the
Northwest Passage. For more on the connection between
roses and the Northwest Passage, see 'Martin Frobisher'
(page 100) and 'William Baffin' (page 94). Incidentally, all
three explorers also had bays named after them.

'HANSA'
Easy to grow and hard to kill, 'Hansa' bears brightly
colored blooms that emit a strong clove scent.

'TOPAZ JEWEL'
Its freely branching habit has branded this an "untidy"
grower. Along with 'Agnes, 'Topaz Jewel' is one of the few
yellow-toned hybrid rugosas.

'THÉRÈSE BUGNET'
Named by its raiser after a close member of the family.

'SCHNEEZWERG'
Its name means "Snow Dwarf", as suggested by its white
blooms and 3ft (1m) stature.

HYBRID TEA

Say the word "rose," and the image that probably appears in most people's minds is of a long, stately stem bearing a symmetrical, formal bloom with a high, pinpoint center: this is a hybrid tea. Their one-bloom-per-long-stem nature makes these the roses of choice for cutting and arranging. Most hybrid teas flower from early spring until late autumn, depending upon the region where they are grown. Hybrid teas are generally upright growers averaging 4 to 6ft (1.2 to 1.6m) in height, making them well suited for planting in the middle of the border. Many rosarians, especially show exhibitors, grow their hybrid teas in special beds where their needs can be met. The lineage of hybrid teas traces back to crosses between hybrid perpetuals (see page 50) and tea roses (see page 66).

'LA FRANCE'

Here is one of the great roses of all time, considered by many to be among the first hybrid teas, if not the very first. Said to be the offspring of 'Mme Victor Verdier' (a hybrid perpetual) and 'Mme Bravy' (a tea), 'La France' was introduced in 1867. Depending on the weather, its flowers may be high-centered, as above, or flatter, recalling its hybrid perpetual ancestors. It finds a place in many rose collections, both public and private.

'TOUCH OF CLASS' OPPOSITE PAGE
This rose won an All-America Rose Selection award in 1983 and is consistently a top exhibition rose in the US, winning Queen of the Show and many other prizes.

'CHERRY BRANDY'
The name was used by its hybridizer twice, once in 1965 (for this rose) and again in 1985.

'FRAGRANT CLOUD'
Translated from its original German name of 'Duftwolke', this rose lives up to its name: it won the James Alexander Gamble Fragrance Medal in 1969.

LEFT TO RIGHT, TOP TO BOTTOM

'OPULENCE'
Originally considered a florist's subject, this rose is
increasing in popularity among home gardeners.

'CRYSTALLINE'
This white beauty is a consistent winner at rose shows.
Its moderately spicy fragrance is a welcome bonus.

'LYNETTE'
Although relatively popular in the US, it is best known
in South Africa.

'SHEER BLISS'
Its attractive pink blush makes this award winner a
popular component of bridal bouquets.

'POLARSTERN'
As its namesake shines in the night sky, this rose's large
blooms stand out in the garden.

'PAUL RICARD'
This rose is licorice scented, a fragrance rarely found in
the rose world.

'ROYAL HIGHNESS'
An award-winning introduction from the hybridizing team
of Swim and Weeks.

'SECRET'
A strong, spicy fragrace graces this pink-edged charmer.

'BRIDE'S DREAM'
This rose grows quite tall and so is best grown in the back
of a border or on a support, such as a trellis.

'FIRST PRIZE'
It often lives up to its name at rose shows by winning
at least a blue ribbon.

'DAINTY BESS'
Not all hybrid teas are full of petals and high-centered!
Although dating back to 1925, this rose remains popular.
Note the distinct maroon stamens.

'SUFFOLK'
Hybridizer Astor Perry named all of his roses after cities
associated with his professional field, the peanut industry.
With this rose he recognized Suffolk, Virginia, the home of
Planter Peanuts.

'ANDREA STELZER'
Andrea Stelzer, the person, was Miss South Africa in 1985
and Miss Germany in 1988.

'PRISTINE'
The name suits it well. Its excellent form has helped it win
at many rose shows since its introduction in 1978.

'JOYFULNESS'
The name is a translation of 'Frohsinn', the name by which
it is known outside the US.

'GEMINI'
Its twin colors recall the sign of the zodiac.

LEFT TO RIGHT, TOP TO BOTTOM

'SILVERADO'
The delicate coloration of this rose conjures up
impressions of the metallic element.

'LYNN ANDERSON'
The name honors the American country/western singer.

'KEEPSAKE'
Shown here as a fully opened flower, this rose does hold
its exhibition form quite well, even in harsh weather.
For its sought-after exhibition form, see page 160.

'MARIJKE KOOPMAN'
Named in the memory of the deceased daughter of the
hybridizer's friend.

'PARADISE'
This award-winning rose combines shades of lavender and
red. The intensity of the colors varies, depending on local
conditions including climate and soil factors.

'LOUISE ESTES'
A noted American rosarian and painter of roses is honored
by this rose.

'BARONNE EDMUND DE ROTHSCHILD'
The baron himself is noted more for rhododendrons
than for roses.

'ELIZABETH TAYLOR'
This classic beauty is named for the legendary actress.

'PEACE'
Perhaps the world's best-known rose, this classic
commemorates the end of World War II. Introduced by
the world-famous Meilland family of France, 'Peace' has
won many international awards.

'ELINA'
Its color varies from medium yellow to almost cream.

'GRACELAND'
Named for the Memphis, Tennessee home of the King of
Rock and Roll, Elvis Presley.

'DUTCH GOLD'
This rose's name celebrates the gold medal award won
at The Hague rose trials.

'ELEGANT BEAUTY'
The sculpturally beautiful blooms on elegant long stems
suggested the rose's name.

'ST PATRICK'
The elusive green cast on its petals is this rose's claim to
fame, as is its worthiness on the show bench.

'POT O' GOLD'
Its flat, open blooms resemble the coins that are said to fill
the legendary pot at the end of the rainbow.

'MRS OAKLEY FISHER'
This fragrant beauty is one of the few single hybrid teas.
See 'Dainty Bess' on page 106 for another example.

LEFT TO RIGHT, TOP TO BOTTOM

'BRANDY'
This is the last rose named by famed hybridizer Herb
Swim. It won an All-America Selection Award in 1982

'FOLKLORE'
This long-stemmed beauty produces remarkable stems up
to 3ft (1m) long.

'TROIKA'
Plum-red new foliage makes an eye-catching contrast to
the flowers, which bloom earlier than many other roses.

'PRINCESS ROYAL'
Its color brings to mind the land of princesses and dreams.

'TOUCH OF CLASS'
Those who grow it, and anyone who sees it, can
appreciate the name.

'HARRY WHEATCROFT'
Named for a noted English nurseryman, this rose's
flamboyant colors match the personality of the man.

'DOLLY PARTON'
Named for the popular country/western singer, these
flowers are flashy and large.

'CAMARA'
Some say this rose glows at sunset.

'DUBLIN'
Your nose will enjoy the uncommon raspberry fragrance.

'OLYMPIAD'
The name commemorates the Summer Olympic Games
held in Los Angeles in 1984.

'DOUBLE DELIGHT'
The blooms of this outstanding variety are a delight
to both the eye and the nose.

'PERFECT MOMENT'
A haunting color combination is produced by
a notably hardy plant.

'TIMELESS'
Durable petals give these blooms staying power in the
garden and in a vase.

'RED DEVIL'
Hybridizer Pat Dickson named this rose in honor of his
comrades in his Royal Air Force squadron.

'DEEP SECRET'
This rose is quite popular in Great Britain.

'MISTER LINCOLN'
Here is a tall-growing rose befitting the American president
for whom it is named. The fragrance and dark red color of
this 1964 introduction make it an enduring favorite. It won
the All America Rose Selection Award 100 years after the
president's death.

LEFT TO RIGHT, TOP TO BOTTOM

'ST PATRICK'
This picture shows the "cycle of bloom" often specified in rose show schedules. From the top are the bud, half-open, and three-quarters open stages that many exhibitors do their best to produce for entry in a rose show. To achieve this, exhibitors grow multiple plants of the same variety, follow special pruning and disbudding schedules, provide all the environmental and cultural conditions the rose plant requires for maximum performance, cut the blooms well ahead of the show date, and use cotton balls to wedge the petals into the perfect arrangement. Of course, every exhibitor has a few tricks not mentioned here to help edge out other competitors. A visit to a rose show, where you will see examples of the very best flowers grown by skilled rosarians, is time well spent.

'ALPINE SUNSET'
The colors of this rose recall a day's end in the Alps. These blooms hold up well in wet weather.

'RUBY WEDDING'
The coloration recalls the precious stone often given in honor of a couple's 40th wedding anniversary.

'CONGRATULATIONS'
The name of this rose suggests its popularity as a gift or as part of the decoration on another gift.

'SILVER WEDDING'
Three different roses have been registered with this name.

HYBRID WICHURANA

These roses, previously classed as "ramblers," are descended from *Rosa wichurana*. This species, native to Japan, eastern China, and Korea, is generally procumbent (flat and spreading) in habit, producing long, relatively thin, pliable canes 20 to 25ft (6 to 7.6m) long. The hybrid wichuranas are a relatively recent group (dating from the 20th century) and provide some of the best landscaping roses suitable for covering large areas, either vertically as climbers or horizontally as groundcovers. They are spectacular when used to cover an arch or trellis or when trained on rope or chain swags.

Most members of this group are characterized by dark, glossy, very healthy and disease-resistant foliage. The small flowers are usually single or semidouble, fragrant, and borne in large clusters, and almost all cultivars are nonrecurrent. Most, however, bloom lavishly during their one glorious flowering period.

'SEAGULL'
For a number of years, this was America's favorite rose in this class. Still popular, a well-grown plant bears thousands of blooms.

'AMERICAN PILLAR' OPPOSITE PAGE
Give this rose plenty of room: it can grow 20ft (6m) in one season. This trait makes it an excellent choice for covering large supports such as arbors and fences.

'NEWPORT FAIRY'
Its name recalls the Newport, Rhode Island home of its hybridizer.

LARGE-FLOWERED CLIMBER

Long, arching canes bearing an abundance of bloom are the distinctive feature of these roses that require plenty of space to perform at their best. With flowers in a variety of shapes, forms, and colors, the large-flowered climbers can be trained to grow along a fence, up the face of a house, on a pergola or trellis, or even up into a tree. Climbers will quickly reach their maximum potential if trained properly and only lightly pruned each year. Their biggest flush of bloom is normally in spring or early summer, with light or mininal flowering during the rest of the season.

'NIGHT LIGHT'
The flowers of this beauty can measure up to five inches across.

'HANDEL'
Noted hybridizer Sam McGredy stated that this is the finest of all the roses he introduced to the gardening world.

'PIERRE DE RONSARD' OPPOSITE PAGE
This rose's namesake was a poet in 16th-century France and Scotland as well as an accomplished gardener.

LEFT TO RIGHT, TOP TO BOTTOM

'BERRIES 'N' CREAM'
The flowers bears the colors evoked by its name.

'RHONDA'
The justly famous 'New Dawn' (see bottom left) is one of the parents of this luscious confection.

'CASINO'
Many rose growers consider this among the best of the yellow climbing roses.

'SILVER MOON'
Unlike most of the rest of the large-flowered climbers, this rose has only one - but magnificent - bloom cycle, which comes early in the season

'SCHOOLGIRL'
Strongly scented flowers open flat.

'DON JUAN'
The dark red cloak (petals) of this heart stealer are reminiscent of the most luxurious velvet.

'LAWINIA'
Sometimes spelled as 'Lavinia', this rose honors the memory of the Duchess of Norfolk (1916 - 1995), who devoted much of her life to charity.

'NEW DAWN'
The first rose patented in the US, this beloved rose can be found growing across much of North America.

'PINK PERPETUE'
Her father is the famous 'New Dawn' (see above).

'POLKA'
Its moderate growth dances nicely up a pillar or post.

'ALTISSIMO' ABOVE
The name means "highest," as in the purest, highest note played in a garden symphony.

'DUBLIN BAY' NEAR RIGHT
Its flowers bloom in waves throughout the season.

'CITY OF YORK' FAR RIGHT TOP
One of an illustrious group of roses honoring cities, many rosarians deem this their favorite white climbing rose.

'COMPASSION' EXTREME RIGHT TOP
This is the most popular climbing rose in England and winner of several international awards. The large blooms are borne singly or in clusters of three.

'AMERICA' FAR RIGHT BOTTOM
This All America Rose Selection winner first appeared in 1976, the year of America's bicentennial. The hybrid tea 'Fragrant Cloud' (see page 104) was its mother and passed along much of her fragrance.

MINIATURE

The smallest of roses in flower size are the miniatures. They range from the tiniest of micro-miniatures, with blooms no bigger than the head of a hat pin, to the medium-sized bloom, and on up to the newest class of minis, the larger mini-flora. Their color range is very wide, from the purest white to almost black-red, with many blends and striped patterns as well. Flower forms run the gamut from single (five-petaled) to high-centered beauties that look just like tiny hybrid teas. There are minis that grow upright, minis with long pliable canes superb for growing in hanging baskets, and even climbing minis that can be trained on a trellis or fence (see the Foreword for a stunning example of 'Jeanne Lajoie'). The plants of some miniatures are very short and compact, while others can become quite tall, emphasizing that the term miniature refers to bloom size rather than bush size. Miniatures make ideal container plants, and many are surprisingly tough and hardy.

'LIPSTICK 'N' LACE'
The artfully applied red edges on the creamy white petals suggested the name of this unusual miniature rose.

'STARINA' OPPOSITE PAGE
The first miniature rose to meet with extensive commercial success, 'Starina' was one the first roses selected for the Miniature Rose Hall of Fame.

'CHELSEA BELLE'
Sometimes a name has a surprising origin: this rose is named for its hybridizer's favorite cocker spaniel, not a woman from New York or London.

'SIMPLEX'
This single (5-petaled) beauty is the epitome of elegance in style and color. Its name means "simple," as in "uncomplicated," in botanical Latin.

LEFT TO RIGHT, TOP TO BOTTOM

'LINVILLE'
Named for a small resort town in the North Carolina mountains.

'IRRESISTIBLE'
Depending on climate, outer petals can show hints of pink or green.

'MINNIE PEARL'
Named for the beloved comedienne of Grand Ole Opry fame, this
rose also brings smiles, especially to those who enter it in shows.

'ROLLER COASTER'
Other flowers on the same plant may be more red than white.

'HURDY GURDY'
At first glance, this little beauty looks like a tiny camellia flower.

'FAIRHOPE'
This is the only rose to date that has received a perfect 10 rating in
the American Rose Society's Roses in Review program. It evokes the
grace of Fairhope, a bayside comunity on Mobile Bay in Alabama.

'JEAN KENNEALLY'
This popular rose was named by a noted rose hybridizer, the late
Dee Bennett, for a friend and fellow rosarian.

'GIGGLES'
This rose's color gives a new meaning to "tickled pink."

'MAGIC CARROUSEL'
It won the first American Rose Society Award of Excellence in 1975.

'LITTLE JACKIE'
Named for one of hybridizer F. Harmon Saville's granddaughters.

'EARTHQUAKE'
Just before this rose was given a name, an earthquake occurred
near the central California nursery that introduced it.

'JUNE LAVER'
Named by hybridizer Keith Laver for his wife.

'INCOGNITO'
This rose's unique color combination captures your attention.

'PEGGY "T"'
The striking red and white petals of this single rose are guaranteed
to make an impression in the garden, in a vase, or in a boutonniere.

'HOT TAMALE'
The name conjures up an image of great heat.

'MY SUNSHINE'
It was nice of the hybridizer to share this little bit of sunshine.

'DAZZLER'
Here is an offspring of the union between 'Kristin' (see page 4)
and 'Rainbow's End', a miniature with red-edged yellow blooms.

'MISS FLIPPINS'
The hybridizer's father named this one for his gymnastically inclined
granddaughter. Also see the contents page.

'OLD GLORY'
The petals are as red as the stripes on the US flag.

'ANYTIME'
This rose easily sets seed, making it a great parent for new roses.

'ORANGE SUNBLAZE' ABOVE
This is the first of the 'Sunblaze' series from the internationally famous Meilland family of France, who also gave 'Peace' to the world of gardeners.

'PETIT FOUR' RIGHT
Here is a rose that is rarely without flowers during the bloom season.

'LITTLE ARTIST' FAR RIGHT TOP
Hybridizer Sam McGredy, famous for his "handpainted" roses, turned his attention from creating larger-flowered roses to produce this little jewel, the first of his hand-painted miniatures.

'ROBIN RED BREAST' FAR RIGHT BOTTOM
This eyecatching extrovert is sometimes grown on a tall, unbranched understock to produce a showy standard (also called a tree rose).

POLYANTHA

The polyanthas are the forerunners to the miniature and floribunda roses. Their small, casual blooms are borne mostly in loose, sometimes large, clusters. Although most polyanthas occur in white or pastel shades, there are a few red ('Mothersday' and 'Verdun'), mauve ('Baby Faurax'), and orange varieties ('Gloria Mundi', 'Margo Koster', and 'Orange Morsdag'). While some polyanthas grow short, compact, and bushy, others grow much taller. Some are small enough to be grown successfully in containers, while others need to be grown in the ground to reach their full potential. Perhaps the most popular of all the polyanthas is 'The Fairy', an easily grown, vigorous plant capable of producing thousands of light pink flowers in one season. It can be pruned almost to the ground in spring to control its potentially large size, or prune it lightly to obtain an impressive plant.

'CHINA DOLL'
Compact and thornless, 'China Doll', like many of its polyantha kin, produces masses of bloom.

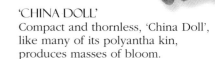

'WHITE PET' OPPOSITE PAGE
This sport of 'Félicité et Perpétue' (see page 72) rewards its grower with clouds of delicate white blooms.

'YESTERDAY'
A newer polyantha (introduced in 1974), the unique lilac-pink coloration of this rose helped it win several gold medals and other prestigious awards.

LEFT TO RIGHT, TOP TO BOTTOM

'RAUBRITTER' ABOVE
Its cascading habit gives the plant, often grown on a support, a graceful air. The cupped blooms resemble one of the classic forms of the bourbon roses (see page 28).

'KATHARINA ZEIMET'
One spray (flower cluster) can bear up to 50 blooms. Its pollen parent (male parent) was 'Marie Pavie' (see below). Also called 'White Baby Rambler."

'CLOTILDE SOUPERT'
At no more than 20in (50cm) tall, 'Clotilde Soupert' makes a fine addition to the front of a rose bed or mixed border.

'LULLABY'
This child of 'Cécile Brünner' (see below) produces very double (75 petals!) pink-flushed white blooms on a compact plant.

'MRS. R. M. FINCH'
Her rosy pink blooms become lighter with age.

'MARIE PAVIÉ'
The small, well-formed buds open into pink-centered white blooms of delicate beauty. 'Marie Pavié' can bloom all year in a fairly warm greenhouse.

'CÉCILE BRÜNNER'
Named for the daughter of respected rose grower Ulrich Brünner, this famous and beloved rose produced a climbing sport that bears large, impressive flower clusters. Its growth resembles that of some tea roses (see page 66).

SHRUB

The shrub roses are truly an eclectic group of roses that vary in more than just bloom color and size. Some are short groundcover types (which share the common characteristics of a low-growing and lax, spreading habit), while others can grow much like climbers in warmer climates (although the same variety might remain only average-sized in cooler regions). They are usually easier to grow than many modern roses, bloom repeatedly, and shed their flowers when spent. An increasingly popular group of shrubs is the David Austin "English" roses, which are the products of an intensive and highly selective breeding program. While most of the them are quite different from each other, they do have a few common traits: the flowers of many are fragrant, most are multipetaled, and they usually have a decorative or casual form as opposed to a more formal high-centered conformation.

'ABRAHAM DARBY' ABOVE
Named for a leader of the English Industrial Revolution, this is one of David Austin's many "English" roses.

'HERITAGE'
This is reputed to be David Austin's favorite of his many rose creations.

'ENGLISH GARDEN' OPPOSITE PAGE
The bloom color of this David Austin rose deepens in hot weather. It grows shorter than many other "English" roses.

'GOLDEN CHERSONESE'
The name refers to a mythical place of wealth and beauty.

LEFT TO RIGHT, TOP TO BOTTOM

ALL OF THESE ROSES ARE DAVID AUSTIN'S "ENGLISH" ROSES

'BELLE STORY'
The name honors one of the first nursing sisters who became an officer in the British Royal Navy in the 1860s. Its growth habits are excellent.

'GRAHAM THOMAS'
Named for one of the greatest contemporary English horticulturists who, among many other achievements, helped revive interest in the old garden roses. Many rate this as one of the finest of all the "English" roses.

'DAPPLE DAWN'
Unlike most other Austin roses, this one is single-flowered.

'CHARLOTTE'
The yellow coloration derives from 'Graham Thomas' (see above) appearing in its background.

'HERO'
This rose bears the name of the mythological priestess of Aphrodite, goddess of beauty. As in some other roses from David Austin, 'Hero' has a myrrhlike fragrance.

'SWEET JULIET'
Many of the English roses are pleasantly scented, and this one carries a classic tea fragrance. Another child of 'Graham Thomas' (above), 'Sweet Juliet' grows vigorously.

'KATHRYN MORLEY'
Its inner petals curve inward within the outer petals to produce a "cup and saucer" appearance. It is named for the deceased daughter of Mr. and Mrs. Eric Morley, who bought the rights to name this rose at a charity auction.

'GLAMIS CASTLE'
This rose bears the name of the childhood home of England's Queen Elizabeth the Queen Mother. The seat of the Scottish Earls of Strathmore and Kinghorne, the castle is the setting for Shakespeare's *Macbeth*.

'TAMORA'
Here is another English rose that clearly shows its old garden rose ancestry in its deeply cupped flower form. It makes a useful addition to a border or bed and shows a high degree of resistance to diseases.

'CONSTANCE SPRY' RIGHT
This is the first of David Austin's "English" roses. Although
it blooms only once a season, its lavish display of scented
flowers places it near the top of many rosarians'
"must-have" list. It is the offspring of a cross between
the hybrid gallica 'Belle Isis' (see page 44) and the
floribunda 'Dainty Maid'.

'SPARRIESHOOP' FAR RIGHT TOP
The name is that of the village where the Kordes nursery
is located (see pages 94 and 140).

'BONICA' FAR RIGHT MIDDLE
This rose is easy to grow and makes an excellent choice
for beginners. More correctly named MEIdomonac, it took
the gardening world by storm after its US introduction in
1987. The first three letters in its correct name inidcate that
this rose was created by the famous Meilland family, who
gave us, among many others, 'Peace' (see page 108), one
of the most famous roses of all time.

'STRETCH JOHNSON' FAR RIGHT BOTTOM
The name honors a noted American Rose Society member.

'COCKTAIL' EXTREME RIGHT TOP
The flowers are sometimes so profuse on this flamboyant
rose that they completely obscure the foliage.

'FIRST LIGHT' EXTREME RIGHT MIDDLE
The delicately colored petals are unusually large.

'DISTANT DRUMS' EXTREME RIGHT BOTTOM
This hardy rose from Dr. Griffith J. Buck of Iowa State
University produces unusually colored blooms with an
intense myrrh fragrance.

'MORDEN CENTENNIAL' ABOVE
This rose is part of a series of varieties bred at the Morden Research Station in Manitoba, Canada. All of the Morden series are extremely cold hardy. In addition, they bloom repeatedly and show good disease resistance.

'HERTFORDSHIRE' NEAR RIGHT
A low-growing shrub from the Kordes nursery in Germany, it bears the name of an English shire (county). It makes a good groundcover.

'CAREFREE BEAUTY' FAR RIGHT TOP
Bred by the renowned hybridizer Dr. Griffith J. Buck, this rose's name describes it well. Blooms up to 4 1/2 inches across adorn sturdy plants for much of the season. One of its parents is Dr. Buck's 'Prairie Princess' (see page 140)

'KENT' EXTREME RIGHT TOP
Here is another groundcover rose that shares a name with an English shire.

'GOLDEN WINGS' FAR RIGHT BOTTOM
Roy Sheperd, author of *The History of the Rose*, hybridized this single-flowered, hardy, vigorous shrub that makes a valuable addition to almost any garden.

'PRAIRIE PRINCESS' ABOVE
Here is one of Dr. Griffith J. Buck's very hardy and
vigorous shrub roses introduced through Iowa State
University. The names of many of his roses begin with
the word 'Prairie'.

'FLUTTERBYE' NEAR RIGHT
Flowers that change from yellow to pinks and golds
make this shrub a multicolored vision of beauty.

'WEISSE AUS SPARRIESHOOP' FAR RIGHT TOP
The name means "White from Sparrieshoop," which is
the name of the Kordes nursery in Germany.
Also see pages 94 and 136.

'TIGRIS' FAR RIGHT BOTTOM
Bearing the name of the Mesopotamian river in Iraq, this
rose is a hybrid of *Rosa* 'Trier', a hybrid multiflora heavily
involved in the ancestry of the hybrid musks (see page
96), and the rarely encountered rose relative *Hulthemia
persica*.

'ORANGES AND LEMONS' EXTREME RIGHT TOP
This flashy shrub carries the "handpainted" signature of
hybridizer Sam McGredy's work. The remarkably red new
foliage provides a strong and attractive contrast to the
aptly named flowers.

'THE SQUIRE' EXTREME RIGHT BOTTOM
David Austin has high praise for the rich crimson to
purple, cupped, heavily fragrant, large blooms of this
thorny bush, another one of his 'English' roses. He also
admits that it does not grow superlatively for everyone,
but success is attainable.

GROWING ROSES

CHOOSING A SITE

Roses are generally sturdy, hardy plants. They will grow under a wide range of conditions except extremes. However, to grow them well, pay careful attention to where and in what they are planted.

Roses prefer at least six hours of direct sunlight. They can tolerate less, but the bushes will be less vigorous, be somewhat leggy (bare at the base), and bloom less. Roses prefer a sandy loam soil, moist but well-drained, with a mix of clay, sand, and organic matter. Most soils are rather low in organic matter, so adding compost or other well-chopped and aged plant or animal material is desirable. Rose roots can probe deeply, so amend the soil at least 2 feet deep. If the soil is very poor, compacted, or rocky, consider growing your roses in raised beds. Roses perform best in soils with a pH (acidity) of 6.0 to 6.5. Soil pH varies dramatically around the country and with gardening practices. A soil pH test every few years will alert gardeners to changes that need correction. Small amounts of dolomitic limestone or pelletized lime will raise pH gradually. Garden sulfur can be used to lower pH.

A HEALTHY BARE-ROOT ROSE
Several strong stems and a well-developed root system will help this plant get off to a strong start in the garden.

BUYING ROSES

All rosebushes are not created equal. In every commercial harvest some plants will be of better quality than others, and this is reflected in the grading system used for roses. No. 1 plants are the best and therefore cost more, while those marked No. 1 1/2 and No. 2 are of progressively less quality and cost less. Although you may have success with nurturing a No. 2 rose, results are normally more satisfying and take less time to achieve with a better grade.

Many newer roses are patented and cost more than non-patented roses or older patented roses whose patents have expired. This does not necessarily mean that the newer patented roses are superior to other roses.

You can buy roses bare-root (dormant plants with all soil removed, and usually leafless), boxed or bagged (generally bare-root plants with peat or a similar material around the roots), or containerized (plants in a suitable soil mix in a pot, often actively growing and sometimes in flower). Whichever form you choose, always look for signs that the plants have not been subjected to extreme temperatures or moisture stress. If buying from a catalog, choose a reputable nursery that offers a guarantee.

A HEALTHY
CONTAINER-GROWN ROSE
Look for topgrowth with unblemished, vigorous leaves and stems. If possible, tip the plant out of the pot to make sure the roots are white.

PLANTING

Roses are sold in two forms: grafted or own-root. Grafted roses, very simply put, are varieties that have been attached by the grower to a more vigorous rose plant, called the understock. A grafted rose is recognized by a knob, known as the "graft union" or "bud union," on top of a short shaft. The canes (stems) of the rose all grow from this knob. In contrast, roses sold as "own-root" are grown from cuttings, and new canes often arise from the roots. Own-root roses will not show a graft union.

Roses that fail the first year often do so because the roots dry out before the rose is planted. This can happen before or after you purchase it. Plant a new rose soon after purchase. If this is not possible, keep the roots moist in a bucket of water or under moist burlap for up to a few days, or you can "heel" the plant in by covering the roots and canes with loose soil in a temporary hole or trench.

To plant a grafted rose, except those purchased in containers late in the season, carefully remove the rose from its container or packaging. Shake loose any packing material used to keep the roots moist. Place the rose in a container of water, covering the roots. Soak the roots for a few hours. Dig a planting hole a little wider and deeper than the extent of the roots. Sprinkle one-half cup of bonemeal or phosphate fertilizer (0-15-0) in the bottom of the hole. If the rose roots fan out in a cone shape, add some soil to the hole to form a mound to support the bush.

Remove the rose from the water. Lightly snip the tips of the roots with pruners; any overly long roots should be shortened to a manageable length. Similarly, shorten the canes to about 6 to 8in (15 to 20cm), cutting just above an outward pointing bud.

Place the rose in the planting hole, checking to see where the graft union is relative to the ground level. In warmer areas, the graft union can be an inch or two above ground level. In colder areas, where the temperature regularly drops below 20° F (-6°C), the graft should be 1 to 2in (2 1/2 to 5cm) below ground level. Add or remove soil from the hole until the graft is at the appropriate level. Supporting the bush in one hand, pull soil into the hole around the roots until the hole is about two-thirds full. Water the planting well to settle the soil, then continue to fill the hole. Form a collar of soil around the bush to hold water, then water the bush again.

Finally, loosely mound soil over the planted bush, covering as much of the length of the canes as you reasonably can. Leave this mound in place for up to six weeks, checking very carefully after the first couple of weeks for signs of growth. Many growers recommend gradually removing the soil mound by hand or with a gentle stream of water from a garden hose. When the mounded soil is removed, the root system should be well established and new shoots should be coming from the canes.

For container roses purchased later in the summer or roses grown on their own roots, planting is a bit different. Their root systems are already established and shouldn't be disturbed any more than necessary. Carefully remove the bush from its container, keeping the root ball intact. If the roots are tightly wrapped around the ball, lightly rub them loose; any large, winding roots should be cut with pruners toward the bottom of the root ball. Set the plant in the planting hole with the graft union at the appropriate level for your climate. Own-root roses can be planted with the top of the root ball level with the ground. Fill the gap around the bush with soil. Water the planting well. With these roses, there is no need to cover the canes.

STEP 1
Prune off any thin, weak growth and shorten overly long canes and roots.

STEP 2
After positioning the rose (see text), fill part-way with soil and water in. Add more soil.

STEP 3
Mound the bottom several inches of the canes with soil brought in from another area.

MULCH

Mulch provides a great deal to a garden. Aside from increasing the attractiveness of the garden in general, the material chosen for mulch can be of great benefit to both the plants and the soil. A heavy (4 to 6in/10 to 15cm) layer of mulch reduces the evaporation of water from the soil, keeping the soil friable (loose and workable) and preventing the soil surface from forming a hard crust. Mulch deters weeds from invading the beds and reduces the effort required to pull them once they have settled in for a visit. When mulch breaks down, it returns organic matter back into the soil, helping to create or retain an open soil structure. Mulch materials can be organic or inorganic. Organic mulches break down into the soil and need to be replenished regularly. These include wood chips, tree bark, chopped leaves, straw, and pine needles. Inorganic mulches seldom need replacing and are in themselves low maintenance, but they can contribute to soil compaction and water runoff. Inorganic mulches include gravel, black plastic sheeting, and landscape, or weed, fabric. Choose a mulch carefully. Water must be able to penetrate; compacted mulch will cause rain to run off and make watering difficult. Landscape fabrics are effective against weeds but prevent the replenishment of the soil by mulch residue. Finally, some mulches deplete the soil of nitrogen as they break down, making an application of nitrogen necessary.

WATER

Any consideration of the care and feeding of roses must begin with water. Water is nature's "service elevator," ferrying nutrients from the root zone and around the rest of the plant. While roses must have water, they do not tolerate flood or drought. A rose will quickly die if the soil around it remains too wet and will wilt if the soil remains dry. Watering needs vary greatly; when and how much depends on climate and soil type, as well as the particular needs of a given kind of plant. Soil should remain moist (but not wet) to a depth of about one foot. This ensures the root system will keep the plant fed, watered, and well anchored throughout the year. Be aware of microclimates and microconditions within your yard: for example, one area may get more rainfall than others, and a spot of sandy soil will drain faster and need more frequent watering than an area of clay soil. Newly planted roses with their unestablished root systems will wilt quickly if not irrigated more often than established plants. Water new roses deeply. Light sprinkling will result in shallow root systems that dry out quickly when the weather turns hot and water becomes scarce. In locations with severe winters, shallow root systems may lift completely out of the ground as the ground freezes and thaws (a process called frost heaving) and so are easily damaged by the cold. Mulching (see above) helps reduce the action of frost heaving, especially if a loose mulch such as pine needles or straw is applied after the soil begins to freeze.

FERTILIZING

If a rose is to grow vigorously and bloom abundantly, it must have nutrients, provided in the form of fertilizer. The choices are many: organic, inorganic, dry, liquid, foliar, time-release, and others. Some fertilizers require more frequent applications; some must be applied in large amounts; some are more expensive; and some are not available in all areas. Organics require soil microorganisms to break them down before the plant can use them. Inorganics, particularly the liquid mixes, are available to the plant immediately but do not last long in the soil. Gardeners should choose a fertilizer that suits their personal method of gardening. Local sources, such as garden centers, nurseries, or feed stores, can answer individual questions.

Roses are heavy feeders; unless using a time-release product, gardeners should apply fertilizer more than once during the season. Applications at intervals of six to eight weeks will usually coincide with the bloom cycles of roses, ensuring their feeding at peak times. Many gardeners apply liquid fertilizer between these scheduled feedings. Before fertilizing a newly planted rose, wait at least three weeks for the plant to establish itself.

Fertilizers are labeled with three numbers, such as 12-12-12. These numbers refer, in order, to the percentage of nitrogen, phosphorus, and potassium. These are the primary elements in any fertilizer. Roses, like other flowering plants, do well with a fertilizer that is a balance of the three or slightly higher in phosphorus.

To complete the feeding, the fertilizer should also contain secondary elements of calcium, magnesium, and sulfur as well as the trace elements boron, chlorine, copper, iron, manganese, molybdenum, and zinc. Whatever the choice of fertilizer, be sure to water it in well after application.

PRUNING/DEADHEADING

Pruning is done throughout the year to shape and control the growth of plants, thereby influencing the amount and direction of growth and the amount of bloom. Pruning tools range from fingers to hand shears, loppers, and saws.

In spring, usually just before the plant breaks dormancy, look for and remove all dead and diseased canes. These will be brown and sometimes shriveled. Next, shorten canes down to the point where the pith (the central spongy-looking material) of the cane is creamy white in color. In colder areas, it is often the case that pruning must continue all the way to the crown of the plant. This is normal and will not normally cause the plant to die. Remove any small, twiggy growth. This growth robs the plant of nutrients that would otherwise be used to produce blooms and should be removed throughout the growing season. Canes growing toward the center of the bush should also be eliminated, the goal being to keep the center open and airy. This promotes good air circulation (reducing the likelihood of some diseases flourishing) and makes it easier to spray a plant with pesticides if necessary. If canes are crossing, remove the weaker one(s), leaving the strongest one to continue growth. Finally, remove any canes that grow in a direction contrary to the desired plant growth pattern, such as canes sticking out from a climbing rose.

Pruning during the growing season is a two-part procedure that continues to shape the plant and, more importantly, controls bloom production. Part one is removing spent blooms, a process referred to as deadheading. The pruning cut should be made about 1/2in (12mm) above a five-leaflet leaf. New growth will emerge from this point. Do not be afraid to prune low on the bush.

Part two is called disbudding and is done soon after the main flower bud emerges from the growing tip.

Many varieties produce several buds close to the end of the cane. When disbudding, you remove the sidebuds, leaving one bud to produce a single, large bloom. Use your finger to remove the sidebuds with a simple pull, pinch, or flick, or use very sharp manicure scissors or a cotton swab.

This type of pruning is a personal choice. Many gardeners prefer not to disbud, resulting in larger numbers of smaller blooms, while others prefer a single, larger bloom, especially on hybrid teas and grandifloras. Many varieties produce sidebuds gradually, making this a repetitive process.

There are a few exceptions to the above guidelines for pruning and disbudding. Most notably:

• Once-blooming climbers and many old garden roses bloom on the last season's growth. In spring, remove only the dead canes. After blooming, you may want to remove petals from spent blooms, leaving the hips (the seed pods that often turn decorative colors as the season progresses). When new growth follows the bloom cycle, prune to shape. With these roses, twiggy shoots on older canes encourage lots of blooms.

• With continuous-blooming climbers and repeat-blooming old garden roses, in addition to the spring removal of dead canes and seasonal shaping, remove spent blooms entirely to encourage repeat blooms.

• Floribundas, polyanthas, and shrubs are cluster-flowered roses, meaning that it is normal for them to produce multiple blooms. Clusters will feature three or more blooms. To force the spray to bloom at one time, pinch out the first, largest bud early. This allows the secondary buds to mature at the same rate.

For more information on pruning and disbudding, particularly for exhibition purposes and on the sometimes subtle differences among the old garden roses, there are many books and other references available. Also, the American Rose Society makes information available through their many publications and programs.

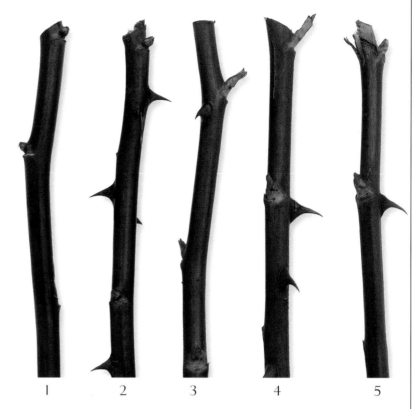

1   2   3   4   5

BAD PRUNING CUTS

1. This cut was made too close to the bud and may cause the bud to dry out or be invaded by disease.
2. Ragged cuts made by dull pruning tools cannot heal cleanly and may provide entry spots for insects and diseases.
3. This cut was made much too high above the bud. The remaining length of cane above the bud will die and leave an unsightly stub.
4. Although made at the correct height above the bud, this cut slopes toward the bud and will direct water toward the bud instead of away.
5. This shows the normal progression of the sort of cut made in picture number 2. Aside from being ugly, it may lead to problems.

MAKING A CORRECT CUT

Make the cut about 1/4in (6mm) above the bud and sloping down from the bud side of the cane. The cut should reveal healthy white pith in the center of the cane; if not, continue making cuts until you see white pith. Learn to make correct pruning cuts by practicing on cut branches or on badly overgrown plants that need drastic treatment.

PRUNING A NEWLY PLANTED ROSE

Developing new shoots on the canes of a newly planted rose often put stress on the unestablished root system. To compensate for this imbalance, it is best to remove some of the topgrowth.

How much of the canes you remove depends on the class of rose and the vigor of the plant you are pruning. As a general rule, the canes of roses that are taller upon maturity are left longer than on shorter-growing plants.

PRUNING AN ESTABLISHED ROSE

Many modern roses, notably hybrid teas, grandifloras, and floribundas, need to be heavily pruned before growth begins in spring. Remove any dead and inward-growing canes, and remove the weaker of two canes that cross.

The aim of spring pruning of established plants is to create a strong and open, manageable framework for the season's growth, so it pays to spend some time on creating an open-centered plant with evenly spaced, healthy canes.

DISBUDDING

PRODUCING LARGER, INDIVIDUAL BLOOMS
As young buds appear, remove all but the top bud on a stem to produce a solitary, large flower. This technique is most often used on hybrid teas and grandifloras, especially for exhibition.

PRODUCING WELL-TIMED CLUSTERS OF BLOOMS
Removing the largest, basically central bud of a developing cluster will encourage the remaining buds to bloom at about the same time. Leave the central bud intact to prolong the display a bit.

DEADHEADING

REMOVING A SUCKER

HYBRID TEAS AND GRANDIFLORAS
Remove fading flowers to encourage the development of a stem bud into another flowering shoot. Cut above a five-leaflet leaf at an outward-facing bud. Many growers stop deadheading once dependably cool.

FLORIBUNDAS
You can remove individual flowers in a cluster as they fade or wait until the entire group has faded. Although more labor intensive, practicing the former choice will keep your garden looking neater than the latter. Make cuts as for hybrid teas.

Suckers are shoots that arise from below the swollen graft union on grafted rose bushes. If allowed to remain, suckers ususally grow more quickly than the desirable top growth and may eventually overwhelm and kill it. The leaves on suckers almost always look different from the top growth; for instance, the leaves have more leaflets or are a different shade of green. To remove a sucker, gently remove the soil down to where the sucker grows from the plant and carefully twist the sucker out and away. If the sucker has grown large and thick, prune it out as closely as you can to the plant. Keep a watchful eye out for further sucker growth.

PEST CONTROL

The first and best defense against pests is a healthy plant. Pests, both diseases and insects, seem uncanny in their ability to sense and attack the weak and stressed plant. Well-fed, well-watered plants, grown in good soil and harboring an arsenal of predator insects, will fend off attacks. Local nurseries and rose societies can recommend varieties that have a reputation for disease resistance.

The second defense is to be observant. Many pest outbreaks can be controlled by early removal of the pest, whether it be squishing small colonies of aphids or picking off leaves with signs of blackspot. Less than total control of insect pests leaves a small population to feed beneficial predators.

When a problem is spotted, you must first identify the cause, then use a control that is specific to the cause. If a pesticide is needed, try the least toxic approach first: insecticidal soap, horticultural oil, or neem oil, for instance. If there is a need to move to stronger chemical controls, limit the application to the affected area. Read and follow the label, and take recommended precautions.

INSECT PESTS

Some insects cause problems, others solve problems, and most can be ignored (or admired). The few that cause rose gardeners the most trauma are aphids, spider mites, thrips, and Japanese beetles.

Large numbers of aphids clustered on a bud can be alarming, but they are usually more unsightly than they are trouble. While the greatest numbers appear in early spring and late fall, their population waxes and wanes through the season as predators consume them. Aphids seem to appear overnight because they reproduce quickly, trying to outpace their predators. Their numbers can be reduced by squishing them or washing them off. Many chemicals will kill them, such as insecticidal soap, horticultural oil, neem oil, or pyrethrins.

Spider mites appear when the days get hot and dry. The first sign of mites is a light speckling on the upper surface of leaves close to the ground, caused by mites feeding on the undersurface of the leaves. A close inspection of the leaves will reveal what seems to be a fine grit: a mix of webbing, dirt, feces, eggs, and mites. Most insecticides will not kill spider mites. The first defense is to spray the undersides of leaves with a forceful stream of water. Insecticidal soap can also be effective. Miticides are available for severe outbreaks; check with a Consulting Rosarian or local extension agent for recommendations.

Thrips are tiny sucking insects that cause damage to flower buds, resulting in malformed blooms, brown petal edges, or failure of blooms to open. Thrips hide within the buds and blooms and are difficult to control. Predators, such as minute pirate bugs and predator thrips, can help keep populations down, but severe outbreaks might call for misting blooms with an insecticide every two or three days until the problem is under control.

Japanese beetles arrive in summer, and for a few weeks the

JAPANESE BEETLES
The bane of many rose growers, these colorful insects can damage buds, blooms, and leaves in a matter of minutes, especially during years where their numbers are large.

garden seems under siege. Some gardeners go as far as covering their blooms with netted bags to exclude the beetles. Hand-picking is the surest manual control. Soil treatments to control larvae, such as milky spore disease, can also be effective. Be careful when using traps: most work by attracting the beetles with sexual chemicals and floral fragrances, so be sure to place the traps at some distance from your roses. Otherwise, you will be advertising a feast for Japanese beetles to attend right in the middle of your rose plantings.

DISEASES

Control of diseases is a preventive activity. Waiting for signs of disease may prove to be too late to control its spread. Good gardening practices are a first step. As with insects, healthy plants resist disease. Plants under stress from drought or those producing rapid growth in response to too much nitrogen fertilizer cannot maintain their natural defenses against disease. Garden cleanup helps reduce disease problems. Fallen leaves left in the garden can spread disease to other bushes or carry over disease spores to the next season, so removing diseased foliage when first seen will help control spread. Although there has been greater emphasis made recently on recognizing and developing disease-resistant roses, do remember that they are resistant, not immune. A regular spray program works wonders to keep disease at bay. A spray program should start as soon as new growth appears in the spring and continue until the roses go dormant in fall. Many spray program options are available. The most intensive and benign is a daily spraying of bushes with water to wash off spores. A bit less labor intensive is to conduct a spray program using a sodium or potassium bicarbonate product or an antitranspirant, generally once a week, or more often depending on weather and plant growth. There are also a number of fungicides that can be applied.

Blackspot and powdery mildew are the most common rose diseases. Blackspot, characterized by black blotches and yellowed leaves, quickly defoliates and weakens the bush. Blackspot appears in warm weather in late spring and summer, generally starting on older leaves at the base of the plant. Powdery mildew, characterized by a white fuzz on leaves and buds, deforms new growth and blooms. It appears in cool, humid weather in spring and fall, usually attacking new growth. Downy mildew, spot anthracnose, and rust are other diseases common in various parts of the country. For specific treatments, contact a local Consulting Rosarian, extension agent, or other expert.

SPRAYING

Gardeners should choose a sprayer appropriate for their garden. Nothing makes spraying a tedious task more quickly than needing to refill a sprayer several times. When spraying, follow directions on the product label and wear protective clothing, covering arms and legs, and wear a hat. If the label recommends it, wear goggles and a respirator. Spray the entire bush, taking special care to spray the leaf undersides, where many disease organisms lurk. Be aware of spray drift, which may damage other plants; spray only on calm days or early in the morning.

WINTER PROTECTION

In warmer climates, roses require little or no protection from cold weather. However, rose growers in areas where the temperature regularly dips below 25°F (-4°C) should take some precautions. A soil, compost, or mulch mound 6 to 8in (15 to 20cm) high, heaped over the graft and up the canes, will provide protection in most areas. In very cold areas, adding a collar of wire fencing filed with leaves around the soil mound provides additional protection. Several styles of protective cones and covers are available commercially. Tree roses, also called rose standards, have a graft at the soil level and a second graft at the top of a shaft. Both grafts must be protected from cold. Depending on the severity of your winters, wrap the top graft with burlap, or loosen and tip the entire plant into a trench. If growing in a container, plant and pot can be moved to a protected area such as a shed or garage. Do not let the roots dry out.

ROSES IN CONTAINERS

Roses can grow very well in containers. Choose a container big enough for the rose: a regular rose will need at least a 15-gallon container; a miniature rose a 3- to 7-gallon container. Terracotta and wood containers tend to draw off water, requiring more frequent watering than plastic containers. Add drainage holes if the container does not already have some. Repot a container rose every three years, changing the soil. Regular watering keeps the potting soil moist; if allowed to dry out, the soil will shed water. Feeding should be lighter than garden roses, but more often. If using a soilless potting mix, use chemical fertilizers, since soilless mixes have no soil organisms to break down organic materials.

Roots of container roses are exposed to weather extremes. Direct summer sunlight can heat up black pots quickly, damaging tender roots. Winter cold can freeze container roots and severely damage or kill a bush. For winter protection, surround the pot with bubble wrap or leaves, bury containers to the lip of the pot, or overwinter them in a protected area.

DOING DOUBLE DUTY
'Flower Carpet Pink' is grown here as both a standard ("tree") rose and as a more conventional container subject. The appeal is obvious.

ARRANGING WITH ROSES

Roses have been used to decorate homes, public spaces, and places of worship since the beginning of recorded history. Both written and pictorial records depict roses in many settings: as a single, perfect blossom as part of a Japanese tea ceremony, in big, voluptuous mass arrangements in the European style, in simple garden bouquets from Colonial times, in floral tributes and bridal bouquets, and in modern American garden club exhibits.

Roses are the ideal flower for arrangements. No other blossom offers as much durability, symbolism, or range of form, color, size, and fragrance. While hybrid teas are the most commonly available commercial cut rose, arrangers should not overlook the creative possibilities of using miniature roses, clusters of floribunda rose sprays, densely petaled old garden roses, or even single roses or rose hips from the garden.

THE STRIPES ARE STARS
Snapdragons, dahlias, larkspur, hypericum berries, variegated English ivy, and maple leaves provide a foil for exotically striped roses. Consider using the bourbon 'Variegata di Bologna' (see page 30) or the floribunda 'Scentimental' (see page 82).

A COLORFUL EXPLOSION
This showcase of exuberance uses zinnias, cockscomb, lilies, trachelium, larkspur, veronica, amaranthus, variegated English ivy, snowberry, viburnum berries and grass to set off pink roses.

Stages of bloom offer additional variety for arranging. From a pointed bud to a fully open bloom of circular form, various degrees of openness of blooms create a sense of movement in an arrangement.

Roses are suitable for all occasions and settings. Their velvety petals, glossy foliage, and sharp prickles ("thorns") provide interesting contrasts with containers of any style and material. Roses in warm hues of red, orange, orange-pink, and yellow go well with wicker baskets, driftwood, pottery, or bronze containers. Roses in cooler colors – white, mauve, and clear pink – are stunning in modern ceramic and glass or antique silver containers. While a simple bouquet of roses or a mass arrangement mixed with other plant materials offers universal appeal, there are many other styles of floral design. Help in learning to create traditional, modern, and Oriental arrangement styles is available through local rose societies or garden clubs. For many excellent ideas, make a point to attend American Rose Society accredited rose shows, which often feature a section devoted to competitive rose arrangements.

WARM AND WELCOME
Make a statement at a dinner party or other gathering with this eyecatching hurricane lamp ring. Yellow hybrid teas add their own heat to a mixture of yarrow, snapdragons, and lime green lady's mantle. Bits of sheet moss provide a textural contrast, and the hurricane lamp and candle provide height and matching color.

SEEING RED
This arrangement is an adaptation of the one at the top of the previous page. Red hybrid teas and smaller red "spray" roses (probably a florist's variety related to the polyanthas or miniatures) are set into a backdrop of variegated English holly, leucadendron stems, English ivy berries, and an assortment of leaves, twigs, bark, cones, and lichen.

RIGHT
This traditional line-mass arrangement arranged by Kathy Noble uses 'Touch of Class' hybrid tea roses and dried reeds for direction and texture. Traditional arrangements are based on basic geometric forms that draw the eye to a focal area located just above the rim of the container.

FAR RIGHT TOP
This miniature line-mass arrangement by Susan Liberta is less than 8in (20cm) tall. All of the design principles that apply to full-size line-mass arrangements are applicable here; only the size of the materials is different.

FAR RIGHT BOTTOM
Dan Faflak made this Oriental-style arrangement with two floribunda roses and some line material. True Ikebana, the Japanese way with flowers, is never judged. However, arrangements designed "in the Oriental manner" (as simple representations of nature's relationship to man) make a beautiful addition to any rose show.

EXTREME RIGHT TOP
Here is a modern free-form arrangement featuring Southwestern colors and textures, arranged by Patricia Freeman, using 'Flaming Beauty' hybrid tea roses. Modern arrangements represent and interpret today's world through the use of bold colors and forms and dynamic lines.

EXTREME RIGHT BOTTOM
A dramatic line arrangement incorporating contemporary line material, arranged by Patricia Freeman, using 'Pristine' hybrid tea roses. This arrangement was staged on a black pedestal against a black background, which creates the impression that it is floating.

DRYING ROSES

The art of dried flower arranging offers a way to enjoy the garden's bounty throughout the year. Of various methods for drying roses, the simplest is to bury them in a desiccant (drying agent) called silica gel. This fine granular substance is sold in craft stores and garden shops under various names and contains blue indicator crystals that turn pink when the granules have absorbed their limit of moisture. The actual process of drying roses is fairly simple and inexpensive. The basic equipment, in addition to the silica gel, includes airtight containers for drying and storage. A wide range of containers is suitable, including cookie tins or plastic shoe boxes sealed with masking tape, or plastic food-storage containers. Other supplies needed are a small, soft artist's brush;

medium-gauge floral wire for standard roses; a fast-drying clear household cement; small plastic dishes saved from powdered drink mixes or single-serving puddings; a clear matte spray sealer; and covered cartons for storage. The silica gel will be the costliest item but may occasionally be found discounted. If drying large-flowered roses, at least five to ten pounds of desiccant will be needed. Miniature roses will require less.

The choice of rose varieties for drying is important, since some dry more successfully than others. Expect changes in color: for example, deep reds may turn nearly black, and most whites become creamy. In between, however, there are many possibilities. Orange-reds dry a rich red; lavender may turn a regal purplish mauve; the contrasting petal edges of varieties such as 'Rainbow's End' become more vivid; and, in general, most colors acquire a deeper hue. Some yellows fade quickly after drying, while others keep their sunny appearance. Flowers should be cut for drying when free of morning dew. They should be conditioned with stem ends in water until the blooms are turgid (not limp) for best results. Roses should be cut in varying degrees of openness

RING OF FIRE
Three colors of dried roses, combined here with poppy pods and amaranthus heads and decorated with fabric, make a cheerful wreath for summer or winter.

from bud to three-quarters open for variety in an arrangement. Avoid fully open blooms, since they tend to shatter (fall apart).

To dry large-flowered roses, cut off stems, leaving about 1 in (2.5cm), into which a 3/4in (2cm) piece of floral wire is inserted. The wire will be used to attach a substitute "stem" to the bloom after drying. Bend the wire at a right angle at the stem end. Stand prepared blooms upright, not touching, in a tin or box holding about 1 1/2in (4cm) of silica gel. Carefully scoop more gel around each bloom to provide support for the outer petals, then gently pour more gel into and over the roses until they are well covered. Seal the container, label with the date and varieties, and put aside. After a week, check the blooms carefully by pouring off the desiccant. If the petals are crisp and the calyx hard, the rose is ready. However, if the calyx is still soft, the bloom should be returned to the container with an inch or so (2.5cm) of silica gel, again face up, and more gel added to bury the calyx only. The box should again be sealed, labeled, and left for three days or until the rose is completely dry.

Following removal from the silica gel, each bloom should be carefully brushed with a soft artist's brush to remove all traces of desiccant from the petals. This step is important, since any left on the petals can reabsorb moisture from the air and transfer it to the flower, causing

BUNCHES OF WARMTH
A basket of air-dried roses in warm colors brings a glow to a room during the dark days of winter.

EASY!
A bunch of dried roses in an antique pot decorated with twine issues a simple statement.

limp petals. Any petals that detach, during either drying or cleaning, may be reattached using a quick-drying cement. Allow them to dry before storing them Miniature roses that have been dried on their own stems create a more natural appearance in an arrangement than "stems" of taped floral wire, and mini rose stems are surprisingly sturdy. Miniatures should be cut with stems of varying lengths from 4 to 8in (10 to 20cm), depending on variety and degree of openness. The buds should have longer stems when possible, since they will occupy the upper and outer areas of the arrangements. Miniatures may be dried on their own stems horizontally in small, sealable containers. Begin by pouring 1/4in (6mm) or more of silica gel in the bottom of the container. Lay the roses in the box, with most leaves removed, and not touching. As with the larger roses, scoop enough gel around the blooms to support the outer petals, continuing to cover them until they are nearly buried. Gently shake the box back and forth to ease the desiccant between the petals, then continue to add silica gel until the

SMALL BUT POWERFUL
Although only a few inches high, this arrangement of miniature roses and accent material catches the eye.

roses are completely covered. If the container is deep enough, additional layers may be added. Seal, label, and set the box aside. Some miniatures require only four or five days to dry, while others take more than a week. Test as for the larger roses. When the roses have been removed from the gel and brushed free of residue, they are ready for use or storage. For storing larger roses, choose a clean, airtight container of ample depth. Cut a sheet of plastic foam or floral foam to fit inside the container. To retard damage from humidity, cut a hollow to snugly accommodate a small plastic dish filled with silica gel. Insert the dried roses, with their wires straightened, into the foam. Cover, seal, label, and store in a dry, dark place until needed. Covered corrugated cartons are useful for protection from light, which can hasten fading. Miniatures may be stored horizontally in covered clean containers like those in which they were dried, with a small dish of desiccant in one corner. Dried roses will fade with time, although this may give a soft antique effect. To slow the loss of color, a clear spray-on matte sealer may be applied.

OTHER METHODS

Note: climate is a major consideration when drying roses for crafts or decorations. Areas with high humidity will require slightly different techniques than those with low humidity, although the basics are the same. The first and most important step is to start with fresh roses, free from external moisture. If working with damp roses, recut the stems and put them in a vase until the blooms are dry.

• Air Drying — This is the simplest technique. Take 1 foot or so (30cm) of stem when cutting the roses, bundle the stems together, and hang the bundle upside down. In humid areas, hang them in a dark room and allow about two weeks to dry. In dry areas, they should dry in three to four days without the benefit of a dark room.

• Microwave Drying — Use the silica-gel technique described at left, preferably in a glass container. Microwave for three minutes on the high setting; the sides and bottom of the container should be hot upon completion. Large roses and mini roses take about the same amount of time. The advantage of microwave drying is speed, but the disadvantage is that the blooms lose much of their color and become rather brittle.

• Dehydrator Drying — Place as many blooms on the racks of a commercial food dehydrator as space will allow without touching. Set the temperature at 100°F (38°C), then leave the unit running for 24 hours for small and medium-sized blooms. Experiment with temperatures and times for larger roses. The advantages of dehydrator drying are having no silica dust to deal with and more vivid colors. The disadvantages are that the blooms will shrink and the colors will change more than with silica gel.

• There are always ways of using dried roses, even if they haven't dried perfectly. For example, place a lopsided bloom in a wreath or swag with its best side out. Roses that shatter in the drying process can be used for potpourri. If a bloom loses a petal or two when removed from the desiccant, the flower can be reconstructed with glue.

• To avoid hot-glue burns, melt glue in a small electric frypan or similar receptacle and dip the blooms in the glue rather than using a glue gun. To get rid of glue strings on a finished project, quickly pass a hair dryer on high setting over the work; the glue strings will split and disappear.

• To make a dried arrangement last longer, keep it out of direct sunlight as much as possible and out of areas of high humidity, such as the kitchen or bathroom. An older project that has gathered dust can be cleaned with a hand-held vacuum on a low setting or by spraying it at arm's length with a can of hair spray, letting the pressure of the propellant blow away the dust.

GLOSSARY

Anthracnose — a spot fungus similar to *blackspot*, but more common on climbing roses.

Attar of roses — a yellowish oil distilled from rose petals that is used for making perfumes.

Balling — the failure of full, well-developed buds to open.

Bareroot — a rose dug up at the rose nursery field and sold with no soil around its roots.

Basal break — new cane coming from bud union at base of old canes.

Blackspot — a fungus disease recognized by dark spots on leaves, often surrounded with bright yellow tissue, causing debilitation and eventual defoliation.

HIPS
ROSA CANINA

Blind shoot — a stem that terminates without a bloom.

Breaks — new cane growth from dormant buds.

Bud — a potential bloom whose petals have not yet unfurled. Also commonly used term for *budeye.*

Budding — the grafting of a bud into the neck of a rootstock. This is the standard commercial method of propagating roses.

Budeye — a vegetative node found where a leaf joins a stem at a leaf axil. New replacement growth starts at a budeye.

Bud union — enlarged growth above the rootstock where variety was grafted.

Calyx — the green cover of the flower bud, which opens into five sepals.

Cane — stem of a rose plant with leaves, flowers and fruit. New canes are usually green-brown or red. Old canes are brown or grayish with lines.

Chlorosis — yellowing of normally green tissue, often due to unavailability of iron, nitrogen, and other nutrients. Yellow leaves with green veins are a common sign of chlorosis.

Compost — nutrient-rich product of decomposed raw organic matter that can be used as a fertilizer or soil additive.

Consulting Rosarian (CR) — One of a national network of members of the American Rose Society who have been certified to give rose information.

Cross – results of cross-pollination between two different varieties or species of plants.

Crown — see *bud union.*

Crown gall – bacterial disease attacking crown or budhead causing masses of bulbous, corky growth with small thin roots attached.

Cultivar — **culti**vated **var**iety, also called a cross or hybrid. Referred to as "variety" in this book.

Cutting — a piece of stem cut from a plant and used for propagation.

Deadheading – the removal of dead or spent blooms to encourage reblooming.

Dieback — a progressive dying back of a shoot from the tip.

Disbudding — the removal of young flower buds to allow the maximum development of the remaining buds.

Downy mildew — a fungus disease causing irregular purple spots on young leaves and stems during cool, moist conditions; can be fatal to the bush.

Fungicide — a substance used to control disease caused by fungi.

Grafting — the process of joining a stem or bud of one plant onto the stem of another. Widely used to propagate roses and many other woody plants.

Groundcover — an informal name for some shrub roses that are low growing and spreading in habit.

Hip — the fruit (with seeds) of a rose. These form on some roses after the blooms shed their petals.

Hybrid— see *Cross.*

Inflorescence — a cluster of flowers (or one flower) on one stem.

Insecticide — a substance used to control insect pests.

Integrated Pest Management (IPM) — a program that considers the use of biological and other environmentally friendly controls of insects and disease as well as the use of pesticides.

Inorganic fertilizer — fertilizer derived from mineral or chemical substances.

Lateral — a side branch that arises from a main stem.

Miticide — a substance used to control mites.

Mounding — drawing up soil and/or mulch up around the base of plant.

Mulch — covering for soil to conserve moisture, insulate the ground, and prevent weeds.

Organic fertilizer — fertilizer derived from plant or animal substances. Adds organic matter as well as nutrients to the soil.

Own-root — a nongrafted rose plant.

Peduncle — the portion of the stem between bloom and the first leaf.

Pesticide — materials such as insecticides, fungicides, and miticides, used to control pests.

Petal — one of the colorful parts of the flower. See below for petal counts.

pH — a measure of acidity and alkalinity. Neutral is pH 7.0, below is acid, above is alkaline.

Pistil — the female part in the center of the flower.

Pith — the spongy material at the center of the stem. An unripe stem is sometimes described as pithy. Dark pith indicates an unhealthy stem.

Powdery mildew — a fungus disease producing a white, cottony coating on plants which later turns the leaves black and wrinkled, especially during periods of warm days and cool nights.

Prickles — the correct term for rose "thorns."

Pruning — the wise removal of plant parts to obtain a more desirable and productive bush.

Remontant/Remontance — same as *repeat flowering*.

Repeat flowering — the trait of a bush to bear more than one set of blooms in a season.

Rootstock — rose variety with a vigorous root system that will accept grafting from other varieties.

Rosarian — a cultivator of roses.

Scion — a budeye used to propagate roses through grafting.

Sepal — one of the five green coverings of a rose bud. They fold back as the flower opens.

Sport — to change characteristics in a part of the plant, usually with regard to bloom color or plant size. Sported growth can be propagated to produce new varieties.

Stamen — one of the pollen-bearing male parts in the center of the flower. They are usually yellow when fresh and darken as the flower ages.

Sucker — shoots or stems that arise from below the bud union, usually from the rootstock below the soil surface.

Systemic — insecticide or fungicide absorbed into the internal system of the plant.

Thumb pruning — finger pruning; to rub off unwanted buds after pruning.

Understock — see *rootstock*.

QUARTERED
'SOUV DE LA MALMAISON'

FLOWER SHAPES

Blown: normally well-shaped bloom past its best; opened wide to reveal stamens and the rest of the center.

Flat: shallow, low-centered bloom with a small number of petals.

Globular: bloom possessing many petals forming a ball-like flower with a closed center.

High-centered: classical shape of the hybrid tea — long inner petals forming a central cone.

Open-cupped: bloom possessing many petals forming a cuplike flower with an open center.

Pompon: rounded bloom with many short petals regularly arranged.

Quartered: inner petals arranged into four distinct sections rather than forming a cone.

Rosette: flat, low-centered bloom with many short petals that are regularly arranged.

Split–centered: inner petals confused (not regularly arranged), forming an irregular central area.

PETAL COUNTS

Single	5 to 12
Semidouble	13 to 16
Double	17 to 25
Full	26 to 40
Very full	41 and up

INDEX

ACKNOWLEDGMENTS AND ADDRESSES

Special thanks to American Rose Society Staff:
Jennifer Collum, Darlene Kamperman, and Carol Spiers.

Also special thanks to the staff at the Dorling Kindersley Picture Library for their assistance during a difficult time for them.

This book would not have been possible without the dedication of the ARS members whose work appears within its pages. We sincerely appreciate their generosity in sharing their time, talent, and knowledge so that others might discover the beauty of the rose.

The writers: Kitty Belendez, California; Don Julien, Washington; Don Koster, Ohio; Dr. Anthony Liberta, Illinois; Susan Liberta, Illinois; Kathy Center Noble, Texas; Aleene Sinclair, Louisiana; Jeff Wyckoff, Washington; Kathy Wyckoff, Washington; Marily Young, Illinois.

Additional photographers: Dr. Anthony Liberta, Kathy Center Noble (for their arrangement photographs).

Editorial Assistance was provided by the Editorial Advisory Committee of the American Rose Society: Jeff Wyckoff, chairman; Kitty Belendez, Dr. John Dickman, Dr. Anthony Liberta, Robert B. Martin, Jr., and Deb Mock. Additional assistance from Dr. Jim Hering, Bunny Skran, the ARS Old Garden Rose Committee, and G. Michael Shoup, Jr.

Special thanks to the Tournament of Roses Association for providing the information on page 92.

American Rose Society
P.O. Box 30,000
Shreveport, LA 71130
Website: www.ars.org

Texas Rose Rustlers Association
Lucille Idom
13106 Blythe
Houston, TX 77015.
Website: www.texas-rose-rustlers.com

Dallas Area Historical Rose Society
P. O. Box 831448
Richardson, TX 75083-1148.
Website: http://community.dallasnews.com/dmn/theyellowrose

Heritage Rose Foundation
1512 Gorman Street
Raleigh, NC 27606.
E-mail: rosefoun@aol.com.
Website:http://members.aol.com/Rosefoun/hrf.htm